P9-CMY-566

Professional English

English for Science and Engineering

Ivor Williams

THOMSON

Australia • Canada • México • Singapore • United Kingdom • United States

THOMSON

English for Science and Engineering

Ivor Williams

Publisher, Global ELT: Christopher Wenger
Director of Content Development: Anita Raducanu
Director of Product Marketing: Amy Mabley
Editorial Manager: Berta de Llano
International Marketing Manager: Ian Martin
Development Editor: Margarita Matte
Associate Production Editor: Erika Hokanson
Senior Print Buyer: Mary Beth Hennebury

Project Manager: Chrystie Hopkins
Photo Researcher: Alejandra Camarillo
Illustrator: Ignacio (IÒaki) Ochoa Bilbao
Interior Design/Composition: Miriam GÛmez Alvarado, Israel MuÒoz Olmos
Cover Design: Miriam GÛmez Alvarado
Printer: Edwards Brothers

Copyright © 2007 by Thomson ELT, a part of The Thomson Corporation. Thomson and the Star logo are trademarks used herein under license.

All rights reserved. No part of this work covered by the copyright hereon may be reproduced or used in any form or by any means - graphic, electronic, or mechanical, including photocopying, recording, taping, Web distribution or information storage and retrieval systems - without the written permission of the publisher.

Printed in the United States of America.
2 3 4 5 6 7 8 9 10 — 10 09 08 07

For more information contact Thomson ELT, 25 Thomson Place, Boston, Massachusetts 02210 USA, or visit our Internet site at elt.thomson.com

For permission to use material from this text or product, submit a request online at http://www.thomsonrights.com

Any additional questions about permissions can be submitted by email to thomsonrights@thomson.com

ISBN 13: 978-1-4130-2053-3
ISBN 10: 1-4130-2053-4

Library of Congress Control Number: 2006906542

Cover Photo Credits:
© Comstock Images / Alamy

Photo Credits:
© Comstock Images / Alamy: pages 1, 2, 8, 14, 26, 40, 58(right) , 62, 63

© Photos.com / RF: pages 3, 4, 12, 15, 16, 20, 22, 24, 28, 29, 30, 34, 38, 42, 43, 46, 56, 57, 58 (left), 59, 64, 70

Hemera Photo Disk: pages 18, 55

© Adams Picture Library t/a apl / Alamy: page 22 (bottom)

© PhotoSpin, Inc / Alamy: page 44

© Image Source / Alamy: page 48

© Spencer Jarvis: page 32

Contents

To the Teacher

English for Science and Engineering is especially designed for university students at the intermediate level who want to use their English for international communication in professional contexts.

Objective

The purpose of this book is to empower students with the language and life skills they need to carry out their career goals. To this end it provides ample opportunities for students to build awareness and practice the language in real-life scenarios. Its integrated skills approach develops the student's self-confidence to survive and succeed in professional and social encounters within an English-speaking global community.

Content

The book has been designed with a core of 30 lessons plus additional resource sections to provide teachers and course designers with the necessary flexibility for planning a wide variety of courses.

The four skills of listening, speaking, writing, and reading are developed throughout each unit within professional contexts. Emphasis is on developing the life skills students need to deal with situations that they will encounter in the job market.

University students, regardless of their major, will immediately be motivated by the opportunity to prepare for the job market as they practice their English language skills in the following scenarios.

R&D

measuring and comparing R&D activities, putting together an R&D project team, planning an R&D project, developing new products

Design and Testing

resolving design issues, value engineering a product, designing tests, conducting performance tests

Manufacturing and Industry

describing technical processes, analyzing areas of expertise, describing habitual routines and current activities

Quality Control, Safety, and Maintenance

describing maintenance procedures, applying safety measures, running quality control checks

Careers and Management

assessing the job market, getting licensed, building a career

Using the Book

Each content-based unit is divided into six two-page lessons. Each lesson is designed to present, develop and practice job-related skills. (See **Content**.)

Vocabulary

A section with additional content vocabulary for Science and Engineering is included for reference. Teachers may choose to focus on this vocabulary through direct presentation, or may encourage the students to use this section for self-study.

Grammar

There is no direct grammar instruction in the core lessons. However a complete grammar resource has been provided at the end of the book. The grammar resource can serve as a reinforcement of the student's grammar skills. It can be used for self-study or independent practice or the teacher may choose to use material in class to present and practice language skills required by the productive exercises in the different lessons.

The language elements are ordered as they appear in the units. But they may be referred to in any order. Each grammar presentation provides a grammar box or paradigm followed by contextual examples and a practice exercise.

Listening

Many of the workplace scenarios are presented and/or established through the listening contexts. Complete audio scripts and an audio CD have been provided for the student to allow for independent listening practice. Student access to audio scripts and CDs also provides multi-level instruction opportunities in the classroom.

Ongoing Assessment

The five team projects found at the end of every unit, as well as the one-page unit reviews at the end of the book provide ample opportunity for ongoing assessment. Unit tests are provided in the Teacher's Resource Book.

Unit 1

Research and Development

a In pairs or small groups, discuss the questions.

1. In your country, which government department has responsibility for scientific research?

2. Which universities in your country have a strong reputation for scientific research?

b Read and complete the text using the words below.

universities	governments	industries	foundations

Funding for Scientific Research

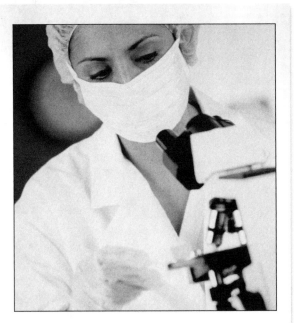

Scientific research requires substantial funding, especially when it involves the use of expensive equipment. This funding often comes directly from (1) _____.
In the U.S. for example, it is the federal government that sponsors most national defense and space exploration projects.

Funding for science can also come from science (2) _____. In 1950, the U.S. Congress passed an act that established the National Science Foundation. This independent federal agency develops a national science policy and supports scientific research and education. Two other well-known foundations that are involved in disease research are the American Cancer Society and the National Heart Association.

Research is also conducted and supported by private-sector (3) _____ that employ scientists—especially from the applied sciences—who work in the development of industrial or commercial processes and products.

Scientific research is also supported by (4) _____ through professorships. Most professors do not just give classes but also conduct scientific research. Indeed, what many professors are looking for is the opportunity to work at a university where they can continue their own research. These are the professors whose students have the chance to observe real research at firsthand. Most universities specialize in certain fields and they are frequently judged on the achievements of their research professors. Scientists whose research findings are published and talked about in scientific circles bring prestige to the institution where they work.

c Read the text again and find the words that mean the same as the following phrases.

1. very large (paragraph 1) _____
2. a law passed by a parliament, congress, etc. (paragraph 2) _____
3. use the services of someone or something (paragraph 3) _____
4. respect and admiration for someone or something of high quality (paragraph 4) _____

💬💭 d In pairs, discuss and write definitions for the following terms from the text. Use a dictionary to help you.

1. the federal government
2. at firsthand

3. the private sector
4. research findings

5. the applied sciences
6. in scientific circles

e Read the last two paragraphs of the text again and complete these sentences.

1. In paragraph 3, line 2, the pronoun *that* refers to _____
2. In paragraph 3, line 4, the pronoun *who* refers to _____
3. In paragraph 4, line 4, the pronoun *what* refers to _____
5. In paragraph 4, line 6, the pronoun *where* refers to _____
4. In paragraph 4, line 8, the pronoun *whose* refers to _____

f Read and complete the sentences with appropriate relative pronouns. The first one has been done for you.

1. It is the Ministry of Science and Education _____*that*_____ decides where to allocate funds.
2. This is the professor _____ book is being published next month.
3. _____ students want is hands-on experience working on real research projects.
4. This is the place _____ decisions about funding are taken.
5. She's the sort of professor _____ encourages students to think for themselves.
6. This is the building _____ most of the research is carried out.

g Complete these sentences with information that reflects your personal views.

1. In this country it is _____ that provides most of the money for scientific research.
2. In my opinion, what science students are looking for is _____.
3. In my opinion, _____ is the scientist whose work has had the greatest impact.
4. The institutions where many scientists want to work are _____.

💬💭 h In small groups, compare and discuss your answers to Exercise **g**.

Lesson 2
Measuring and comparing R&D activity

a Discuss the following questions in pairs or small groups.

1. How can the level of R&D activity of a company be measured?
2. Which measure do you consider to be the best indicator of R&D activity?

b Listen and complete the notes. Check and compare your answers.

CD
T-1

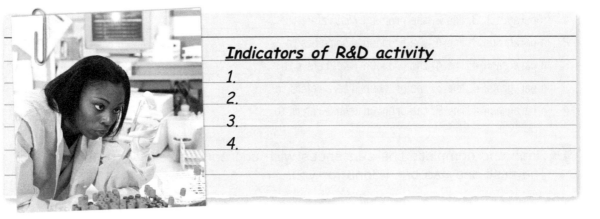

Indicators of R&D activity

1.
2.
3.
4.

c Read the sentences and circle *True* or *False*.

1. The larger the budget, the higher the level of R&D activity.	True	False
2. R&D intensity refers to the total amount of money spent on R&D.	True	False
3. R&D intensity information changes over time.	True	False
4. A high number of publications reflects a high level of R&D activity.	True	False
5. R&D intensity information is confidential.	True	False

d Look at the chart and estimate what percentage of their revenue companies spend on R&D.

Annual R&D expenditure as a percentage of revenue		
1. A typical U.S. industrial company:	_3.5_	% (approx) of revenue
2. A high-tech company, e.g., a computer manufacturer:	_____	% (approx) of revenue
3. U.S. pharmaceutical company Merck & Co.:	_____	% of revenue
4. Swiss pharmaceutical company Novartis:	_____	% of revenue
5. Swedish telecommunications company Ericsson:	_____	% of revenue
6. U.S. pharmaceutical company Allergan (highest spender):	_____	% of revenue

(Source: UK R&D Scoreboard, 2004)

e Listen and check your answers.

CD
T-2

f Read and complete the text with the words from the box.

costs	customer	failure	invest	precision
profit	profitable	R&D-intensive	spenders	unprofitable

The big (1) _____*spenders*_____ in R&D tend to produce certain types of product—things like (2) _____ scientific instruments, medicines, high-tech weapons systems, navigation and safety devices for aircraft, etc. Whereas, typically, a manufacturing company might make a profit of 40% on its sales, the profits of these (3) _____ companies can range from 60% to as high as 90%. In other words, manufacturing (4) _____ represent only 10% of the price that the (5) _____ pays for the product—the remaining 90% being (6) _____. One might ask how these companies can justify figures like these. The explanation lies in the fact that, for them, R&D carries a high risk of (7) _____. A large part of the time and money that they (8) _____ in R&D does not create any (9) _____ products at all. So the high profits of a handful of successful products serve to offset the cost of numerous (10) _____ projects.

g Read the completed text and answer the questions.

1. For a typical manufacturing company, what percentage of sales represents profit? _____
2. In what manufacturing fields do R&D-intensive companies tend to operate?
   _____
3. What percentage of sales is profit for an R&D-intensive company? _____
4. Why is R&D a high-risk activity for some companies?
   _____

h In pairs, role-play a conversation in which a scientist from an R&D-intensive company explains the economics of R&D investment to a layperson.

i In pairs or small groups, look for information on one or more of the topics in the box below and prepare an oral report.

   1. Spending on R&D as a percentage of revenue in the place where you work
   2. Spending on R&D as a percentage of revenue in a well-known company in your country
   3. Reviews, journals, periodicals, etc., where scientists can get their research work published
   4. The largest recipients of funding for research in your country
   5. The process by which inventions and innovations are patented in your country

Lesson 3
Coordinating the members of the team

a Look at the cartoon and, in pairs, discuss what you think it is about.

b Read and complete the text with the connecting phrases from the box. Two of the expressions are in two parts.

as a result
because
in order to
neither / nor
not only / but also
though

Laypeople often think of R&D scientists as solitary figures working in a laboratory on some abstract problem. (1) ___*Though*___ this may be true for a handful of scientists working on basic research, the vast majority work on R&D projects in teams. These project teams include (2) _____ scientists from various disciplines _____ representatives from diverse functional groups within a company, for example, marketing, manufacturing, and human resources.

Formerly, R&D projects were passed from one group of specialists to another in serial fashion. The term "throwing it over the wall" was often used to describe this way of working, in which each stage of the process was isolated from the others. Research evidence showed that this method was (3) _____ efficient _____ cost-effective (4) _____ it was very time-consuming.

Companies now bring together representatives from each stage of the process and, in this way, they try to achieve more cross-functional communication and participation. The goal is to coordinate processes better and to identify and avoid problems that otherwise might only be discovered later. (5) _____ work effectively in cross-functional project teams, scientists must have both up-to-date knowledge of their technical fields and also skill in communication, problem-solving, and group decision-making—all necessary for successful teamwork. (6) _____, universities are now giving more importance to the development of these skills, and companies are looking for ways to foster these attributes in training programs for their employees.

c In pairs, find synonyms for the following hyphenated phrases from the text.

1. cost-effective   2. cross-functional   3. time-consuming   4. up-to-date

_____   _____   _____   _____

d Read through the completed text and answer the questions.

1. According to the text, what is a common misconception about R&D scientists?

   _____

2. What sort of people make up an R&D project team nowadays?

   _____

3. Why is the term "throwing it over the wall" an appropriate one?

   _____

4. What is required of scientists who are working in cross-functional project teams?

   _____

e You have been assigned the task of choosing a project leader for an R&D project. Make notes of the qualities and skills that you think a good project leader should have.

> **R&D project leader**
> - ●   ●   ●
> - ●   ●   ●

f Compare and discuss your answers in pairs.

g Listen to the discussion on choosing a project leader and compare your ideas with those that you hear.

CD
T-3

h Combining your ideas with those that you heard in the conversation, complete the sentences describing the ideal qualities of a project leader. Add sentences of your own.

The ideal project leader is a person who _____

Ideally, the project leader should _____

_____

_____

_____

History capsule

The earliest R&D laboratories were founded at the end of the nineteenth century in Germany by companies like Siemens, Krupp, and Zeiss. It was not until the years immediately preceding World War I that the major American companies started to take research seriously. It was during this time that Du Pont, General Electric, AT&T, Eastman Kodak, Westinghouse, and Standard Oil established laboratories for the first time.

Lesson 4
Working out a logical sequence

 a Discuss the questions in pairs or small groups.

1. What sort of projects are you sometimes required to plan?

2. How do you plan a project?

3. Do you consider yourself to be a good planner?

4. What skills are required when planning a project?

b Listen to the interview about research and development projects and complete the notes.

CD
T-4

1. The letters CPM stand for:

2. CPM is used to determine:

3. Timescale:

4. "Slack time":

5. Allocation of resources:

c Look at the words and phrases from the interview. Match each verb with the correct noun or noun phrase to form appropriate collocations.

1. work out   _e_   a. resources

2. construct   _____   b. a timescale for a project

3. add up   _____   c. a delay

4. establish   _____   d. the total number of weeks

5. allocate   _____   e. a logical sequence

6. cause   _____   f. a diagram

d Look at the diagram and circle the correct options.

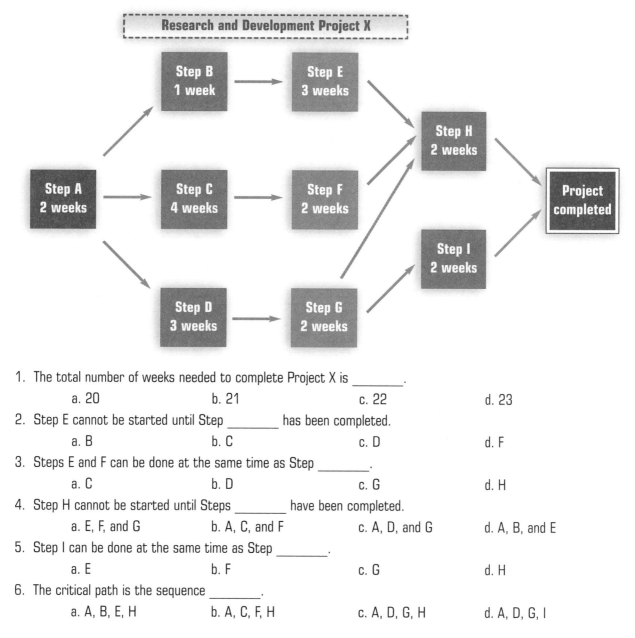

Research and Development Project X

1. The total number of weeks needed to complete Project X is _____.
   a. 20   b. 21   c. 22   d. 23
2. Step E cannot be started until Step _____ has been completed.
   a. B   b. C   c. D   d. F
3. Steps E and F can be done at the same time as Step _____.
   a. C   b. D   c. G   d. H
4. Step H cannot be started until Steps _____ have been completed.
   a. E, F, and G   b. A, C, and F   c. A, D, and G   d. A, B, and E
5. Step I can be done at the same time as Step _____.
   a. E   b. F   c. G   d. H
6. The critical path is the sequence _____.
   a. A, B, E, H   b. A, C, F, H   c. A, D, G, H   d. A, D, G, I

e In small groups, invent an R&D project and prepare a list of tasks that will have to be completed during the project. Include between eight and twelve steps, but do not include time allocations. Then pass your list to another group.

f Read through the other group's list of tasks and allocate a minimum time (in weeks) for the completion of each step and write this on the list. Then pass your list to another, different group.

g Read through the other group's list of tasks and time allocations and prepare a Critical Path diagram to show the minimum number of weeks that will be needed to complete the entire R&D project.

Lesson 5

Gradually increasing expenditure

a Discuss the questions.

1. How often do you have to handle or present data in the form of graphs?
2. What other visual aids do you use to present information?

CD
T-5

b Listen to the lecturer and label the graphs with the correct numbers. Then listen again and complete the sentences.

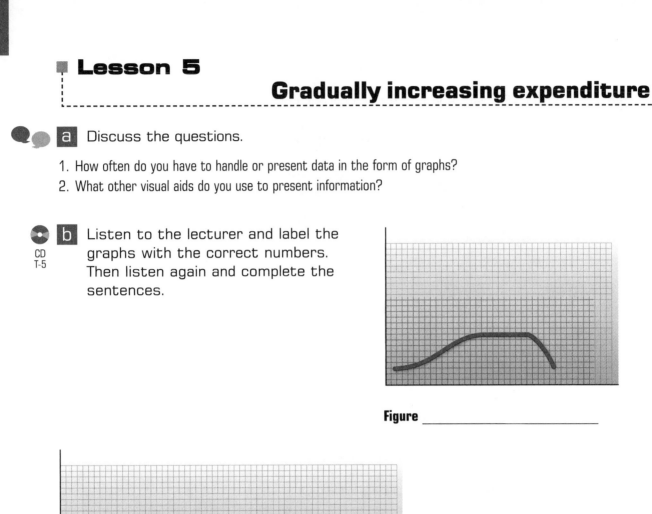

Figure _____

Figure _____

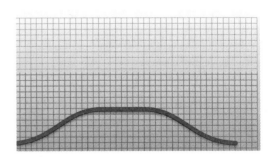

Figure _____

1. In the early stages of a typical project, R&D expenditure _____
2. Sales usually fall gradually as _____
3. Sales can fall abruptly if _____
4. Ideally, a company aims to operate a number of projects, _____

c Complete each sentence by matching it with the appropriate ending.

1. R&D planning consists of choosing projects that (1)_____
2. Managers have to make sure that the total effort needed to carry out an R&D project is (2)_____
3. If it is greater (3) _____
4. If it is significantly less (4) _____
5. So, managers have to be sure that the demands on their capacity and their resources are (5)_____
6. To maintain a balanced situation (6) _____
7. Each proposal must be studied by (7) _____
8. And R&D managers have an important role to play in proposing new projects (8)_____

a. enough to keep them fully loaded but not overloaded.

b. there needs to be a steady flow of new R&D proposals.

c. will use available human and financial resources in the most efficient and profitable way.

d. they will not be working to their fullest capacity.

e. as well as in carrying them out.

f. they will not be able to reach established targets.

g. experts in technical, commercial, financial, and manufacturing areas.

h. neither greater nor significantly less than the resources that they have available.

d Work in pairs. Role-play conversations based on the following information.

Student A: You are R&D project manager for Teknik, Inc. Choose one of the problems below, present it to Student B, a senior manager, and discuss possible ways to improve the situation.

Student B: You work for Teknik, Inc. in senior management. Listen to Student A's problem and then discuss possible ways to improve the situation.

Option 1
You have two products in initial phases of development. They are not yet ready for production. The company also has a product on the market that has been successful but that is now out-of-date and is losing sales.

Option 2
Your company is enjoying very good sales on two recently launched products and it has another product that is now suffering from obsolescence and consequently is losing market share.

e Write an account of the problem and solution(s) that you and your partner discussed in the previous exercise.

The problem is that the company has not invested enough in . . .

Lesson 6

Developing a new product

a Discuss these questions in small groups.

1. How does the R&D department of a company generate ideas?

2. How does it test ideas?

CD
T-6
b Listen to someone from an R&D department and complete the notes. Check and compare your answers.

1. *Generating ideas*

_____

_____

_____

_____

2. *Testing ideas*

_____

_____

_____

_____

c Read each sentence and circle the correct option.

1. To "screen" ideas means to test them in order to . . .

    a. prove they work.   b. see how much they cost.   c. discard those that are no good.

2. An "unsound" concept is . . .

    a. untested.   b. old-fashioned.   c. faulty.

3. "Key" questions are . . .

    a. urgent.   b. fundamental.   c. complicated.

4. If something is "technically feasible", it . . .

    a. can be done.   b. should not be done.   c. should be done.

5. "Prospective" customers are . . .

    a. loyal customers.   b. doubtful customers.   c. likely customers.

d In pairs, role-play a conversation about what you have learned so far about how ideas are generated and tested. One student plays the part of an expert and the other is a layperson.

e Complete the text with words from the box.

before	essential	expensive	fuzzy	money	product
serious	sound	time	total		

We call this whole "getting started" period the "(1) _____*fuzzy*_____ front end." It's usually not a very (2) _____ part of the process but it can take up to 50% of total development (3) _____. This is where we decide on a clear, (4) _____ concept and make (5) _____ commitments regarding time, (6) _____, and how the (7) _____ will be.

Some people consider this phase as something that happens (8) _____ development. But I prefer to think of it as an (9) _____ part of development and I include the time that we need for this as part of the (10) _____ development cycle time.

f Listen to check your answers.

CD
T-7

g Answer the questions about the text.

1. Why do you think R&D scientists refer to this period as the "fuzzy front end"?

   _____

2. Why do you think that the fuzzy front end can sometimes take up so much time?

   _____

3. In your opinion, should the fuzzy front end be considered as part of development or something that happens beforehand?

   _____

h Discuss your answers with a classmate.

i Work in small groups. Choose one of these topics and discuss it in your group.

1. You have been asked to reduce the length of the fuzzy front end of your R&D development process. What do you propose?	2. You have been asked to sound out potential customers about an idea for a new product. What questions will you ask them?

j Discuss these questions in small groups.

1. What techniques do you use to generate ideas?
2. Which techniques work best for you?
3. Which of these techniques could be applied to product development in an R&D department?

Team Project 1

Task:
Plan an R&D Project

You work in the R&D department of a large manufacturing company that makes a wide variety of high-tech products. It is your job to present proposals for new R&D projects.

With your team:

1. Decide on a subject for your R&D project.

2. Select the techniques that you will use to generate ideas.

3. Decide how you will test those ideas.

4. Write a short description of the aims of your R&D project.

5. Write a list of the members of your project team and their specific areas of expertise.

6. Write a description of the areas of responsibility of the project leader.

7. Taking into account "fuzzy front end" time, use CPM or some other method to determine a timescale for the project.

8. Give a presentation of your finished R&D proposal complete with any relevant diagrams, graphs, charts, tables, etc.

Unit 2

Design and Testing

a Look at the photos and discuss the questions in pairs.

1. What do you think all these items have in common?

2. When do you think each of these items was designed?

b Listen and complete the summary of the life of Raymond Loewy. Then listen again and complete the notes below with examples of Loewy designs.

CD T-8

1893	• *Raymond Loewy is born in Paris, France*	
1918	• receives degree in electrical engineering	
1919		
	• receives first industrial design commission • starts his own design firm	
1934		
from 1937	• designs streamlined styling of passenger trains for Pennsylvania Railroad	
1930s and 40s	• designs wide variety of household products, rounded corners and simplified lines, e.g., *Frigidaire* refrigerators and freezers	
	• forms Raymond Loewy Associates	
1954		
	• redesigns Coca-Cola bottle	
1960		
1961	• designs Avanti sports car for Studebaker	
	• designs five cent U.S. postage stamp, John F. Kennedy	
1967–73		
1971	• designs Shell logo	

Greyhound *Scenicruiser*

Studebaker *Avanti*

Shell logo

Skylab

1. household consumer goods: *refrigerators,* _____

2. transportation: _____

3. soft drinks: _____

4. miscellaneous: _____

C Read the sentences and circle each *True* or *False*.

1. By 1920, Loewy had already left France.   True   False
2. By 1940, Loewy had worked for the Pennsylvania Railroad.   True   False
3. By 1958, he had designed both bottles and cans for Coca-Cola.   True   False
4. When he designed the *Avanti,* he had already designed other cars.   True   False
5. By 1928, Loewy had established his own design firm.   True   False
6. By 1965, Loewy had started working for NASA.   True   False
7. By the 1970s, Loewy had even designed postage stamps.   True   False

d Read the text and complete each space with the correct form of the verb in parentheses.

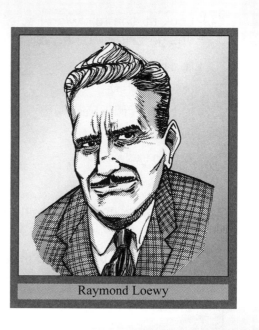

Through his accomplishments in product design, Raymond Loewy (1) ___*helped*___ (help) to establish industrial design as a profession. By the end of his life, his career (2) _____ (encompass) all applications of modern industrial design, from consumer products to interior building space, packaging, and transportation.

Long before his death, Loewy (3) _____ (become) one of the best known industrial designers of the twentieth century and his vision of beauty through the use of streamlined, highly functional forms (4) _____ (shape) modern industrial design in the United States. For decades, his work (5) _____ (permeate) the nation's lifestyle and influenced—and (6) _____ (continue) to influence today—countless aspects of American life.

Raymond Loewy

e Discuss these questions in pairs or small groups.

1. In your opinion, what were Loewy's most impressive design achievements?
2. Where can Loewy's influence on the world of industrial design still be seen?
3. What does Loewy's career reveal about the work of an industrial designer?
4. What aspects of industrial design do you find most and least appealing?

f Research and prepare an illustrated written report about a well-known present-day industrial designer from your own country or from abroad.

Lesson 2
No single, unified style of industrial design

a Read and discuss the text in small groups.

According to currently prevailing standards of industrial design, a product, apart from being cost-effective in its use of resources, should satisfy the following criteria, though the relative importance of any of these standards will vary depending on the object:
- ✔ expression of function in terms of form
- ✔ beauty of line, color, proportion, and texture
- ✔ convenience and/or comfort in use
- ✔ high efficiency and safety of operation
- ✔ durability
- ✔ ease of maintenance and repair

b Look at the following list of products and, for each one, write the industrial design criteria that you think would have, relatively, more importance.

1. a lawn mower: _____
2. an office desk lamp: _____
3. a garbage collection truck: _____
4. a mobile phone: _____
5. a washing machine: _____

c Discuss your answers in pairs.

d Look at the photos and answer the questions in pairs.

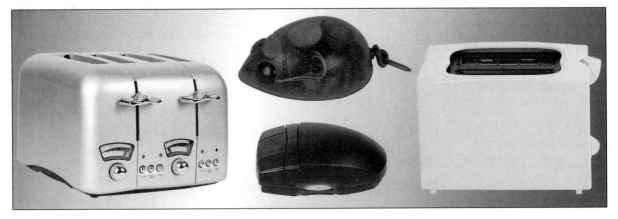

1. Which computer mouse do you prefer and why?
2. Which toaster do you prefer and why?
3. What design improvements, if any, would you suggest for either item?

e You are going to hear someone talking about four trends in industrial design. Listen and number the topics in the order that they are discussed. Four of the topics below are not mentioned. Then listen again and take notes of the positive views expressed about each topic.

CD
T-9

- ☐ the origins of industrial design
- ☐ artificially accelerated obsolescence
- ☐ packaging
- ☐ the cost of industrial design

- ☐ an emphasis on impersonality
- ☐ the role of art in design
- ☐ "classics" of industrial design
- ☐ streamlining

	Positive point of view	Negative point of view
Topic 1		
Topic 2		
Topic 3		
Topic 4		

f Now listen to another speaker offering a contrasting point of view and complete the rest of the chart.

CD
T-10

g In small groups, debate the merits of the two speakers' respective points of view.

h Write an article about the way you think industrial design will change in the future.

History capsule

German architect and designer Peter Behrens (1868–1940) is considered by many to be the first industrial designer. In 1907, he created the entire corporate identity for AEG. Among his students were architects and designers like Walter Gropius, Mies van der Rohe, and Le Corbusier.

Lesson 3
Compromises and engineering designs

a In pairs or small groups, discuss the questions.

1. What does the word "dilemma" mean?
2. What sorts of dilemmas might you face in your studies or in your work?
3. What do you understand by the term "trilemma"?

b Work in groups of three. You are part of a software design team. Read the information on the role cards and assign one card to each person in your group.

Designer 1	Designer 2	Designer 3
You want to make a low-cost educational computer game and you want to bring it to market quickly.	You want to make a high-quality and low-cost educational computer game.	You want to make a high-quality educational computer game and you want to bring it to market quickly.

c Working alone, make notes about the software product you want to make.

This computer game will have a low cost. We will try to launch it by . . .

d Work again in the same group of three. Take turns sharing your ideas with the other members of your group.

e Complete the sentences to explain the software economics "trilemma."

1. You can make a high-quality product and you can bring it to market quickly, but . . .

_____

2. You can make a high quality, low-cost product, but . . .

_____

3. You can make a low-cost product and you can bring it to market quickly, but . . .

_____

f Complete the text with the nouns in the box. There are two extra words.

compromises	costs	designs	engineers	markets	mathematics
	merits	models	requirements	solutions	

(1) _Engineers_ use their knowledge of science and (2) _____, along with their own relevant experience, to find a suitable solution or solutions to a problem. They create appropriate mathematical (3) _____ of a problem, they analyze it, and then test potential (4) _____. Usually there are a number of reasonable solutions to a problem. So, engineers evaluate each design option on its (5) _____ and choose the solution that best meets their (6) _____. (7) _____ are at the heart of all engineering (8) _____. The "best" design is the one that meets as many of the given requirements as possible.

g Discuss the text and how these principles apply to your studies or to your work.

h You have been assigned the task of designing a new hand-held computer game device. First, complete the lists of desirable design values with the correct nouns and adjectives.

noun / noun phrase	adjective / adjective phrase
(1) *durability*	durable
attractiveness	(2)
low cost	low-cost
(3)	reliable
safety	(4)

noun / noun phrase	adjective / adjective phrase
high quality	(5)
(6)	efficient
ease of use	easy to use
(7)	compact
light weight	(8)

i Add any other desirable design values that you think are relevant to this product.

j Work in groups. Discuss the ways in which one design characteristic might conflict with others and the design compromises you would have to make.

If we make it more durable, that will increase the weight and also the cost.

But if we make it more lightweight, it won't be so strong.

k Share the conclusions of your group's discussion with the rest of the class.

Lesson 4

Value engineering

a Discuss the questions in pairs or small groups.

1. What do you understand by the term "value engineering"?
2. When did engineers first start to apply principles of value engineering?
3. How do engineers value engineer a product?

CD
T-11

b Listen to an interview about value engineering and complete the notes. Check and compare your answers. Then listen again and circle the statements *True* or *False*.

Value Engineering
_____
_____
_____
_____

Value
_____
_____
_____
_____

Origin of the concept
_____
_____
_____
_____

Applying value engineering
*1.*_____
*2.*_____
*3.*_____
*4.*_____

1. Value engineering came about as a consequence of World War II.	True	False
2. Value can be increased either by improving function or by increasing cost.	True	False
3. The first step in value engineering is an analysis of a product's functions.	True	False
4. It is acceptable to sacrifice quality in the quest for better value.	True	False
5. In the final step, findings are presented and recommendations are made.	True	False

c Correct the false statements.

d Read the text and fill in the correct heading for each paragraph.

cheaper substitute materials	customer feedback	efficiency and producibility
efficient use of energy	modules and subassemblies	

Value engineering looks to optimizing costs by eliminating wasteful practices. How does it do this?

1. _____*efficient use of energy*_____: Reduce costs and add value to a product by making it more energy-efficient.

2. _____: Replace expensive materials with cheaper ones that function just as well. If a product is only expected to last for ten years, it is wasteful to use materials that last much longer. In a perfectly value-engineered product, all materials wear out at the same time.

3. _____: Redesign products to make them more producible and adopt more efficient production processes. Eliminate unnecessary parts, unnecessary standards of precision, and any unnecessary steps in the production process.

4. _____: Use multipurpose components that can be reused in a number of slightly different products. In this way, save on original engineering and design costs.

5. _____: A product that has more features than customers actually want is wasteful and inefficient. Redesign a product so that it matches exactly what most customers want. Extras can then be sold as options.

e In small groups, think of at least one real-life example for each of the value engineering practices mentioned above. Make a list.

f Read about these real-life cases and, in small groups, discuss which of the value engineering principles listed in the box are being applied in each case.

reduce unnecessary parts	use cheaper substitute materials	reduce unnecessary precision

1. As long as they do not leak, the welded joints on Russian rocket motors are allowed to look ugly. Grinding and finishing the welds adds cost but does not make the motors function any better.
2. Many car manufacturers actively look to reducing the numbers and types of fasteners that they use. The aim is to reduce the costs of inventory, tooling, and assembly.
3. Japanese manufacturers of printed circuit boards use phenolic resin and even paper to reduce costs. They also use just one or two copper layers but without affecting the quality of the finished product.
4. On some computer circuit boards, the conductors are made in such a way that they also act as resistors and inductors as well, thus eliminating the need to include these components.
5. The accepted margin for disc brake components on some Japanese cars is 3 millimeters, which is not at all difficult to achieve. Even with this level of tolerance, fewer than one in a million parts do not fit.

g In pairs, role-play a discussion about how to value engineer a product.

Lesson 5

Testing your products

a Discuss the questions in pairs or in small groups.

1. What were/are your favorite computer games? Why?
2. What other software products besides games do you rate highly?
3. What changes have you observed in computer games over the years?
4. How do you think computer games will develop in the near future?

b Listen to the interview and take notes about the three main types of playtests.

CD
T-12

Playtests

1.

2.

3.

c In groups, brainstorm initial ideas for testing a new software product. Use the suggestions in the box or your own ideas.

a race game
a sports game
a multimedia encyclopedia on CD-ROM
a role-playing game
a multimedia dictionary on CD-ROM
language learning software

To test the dictionary, I think we should select members of the public of different ages . . .

d Now write a list of specific questions to ask a tester who does not have any specialized technical knowledge.

Did you find it easy to understand the instructions?

e In pairs, role-play an interview between a software designer and a member of the public who has just tried a test copy of a new game, CD-ROM, etc.

What did you think of the graphics?

f Read and number the paragraphs in the correct order.

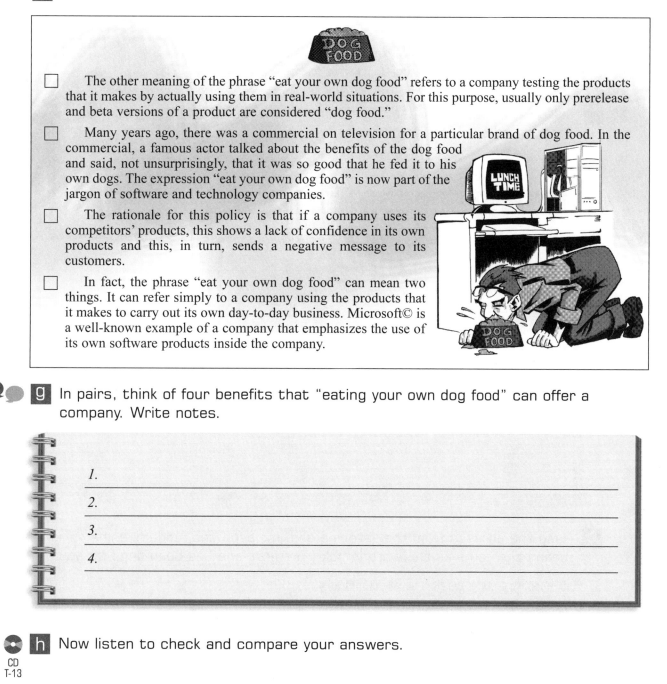

☐ The other meaning of the phrase "eat your own dog food" refers to a company testing the products that it makes by actually using them in real-world situations. For this purpose, usually only prerelease and beta versions of a product are considered "dog food."

☐ Many years ago, there was a commercial on television for a particular brand of dog food. In the commercial, a famous actor talked about the benefits of the dog food and said, not unsurprisingly, that it was so good that he fed it to his own dogs. The expression "eat your own dog food" is now part of the jargon of software and technology companies.

☐ The rationale for this policy is that if a company uses its competitors' products, this shows a lack of confidence in its own products and this, in turn, sends a negative message to its customers.

☐ In fact, the phrase "eat your own dog food" can mean two things. It can refer simply to a company using the products that it makes to carry out its own day-to-day business. Microsoft© is a well-known example of a company that emphasizes the use of its own software products inside the company.

g In pairs, think of four benefits that "eating your own dog food" can offer a company. Write notes.

1. _____
2. _____
3. _____
4. _____

h Now listen to check and compare your answers.

CD
T-13

i Discuss the questions in pairs or small groups.

1. Is the "eat your own dog food" concept only relevant in software and technology companies?
2. How can this concept be applied in other areas of science and engineering?
3. Are there any potential drawbacks to the "eat your own dog food" concept?

j Research and prepare a report about the testing procedures used in a company in your country.

Lesson 6
Choosing to performance test products

a Discuss the questions in pairs.

1. What is the difference between safety testing and performance testing?

2. Why do companies conduct safety testing and performance testing?

b Listen to an interview about performance
testing and complete the notes.

CD
T-14

1. Difference between safety testing and performance testing

_____

2. Reasons for conducting performance testing

_____

   internal test data:

_____

   comparison with competitors' products:

_____

   marketing claims:

_____

   endorsements:

_____

   retailers:

_____

c Read the phrases from the listening and, for each one, underline the option that means the same as the word in bold. The first one has been done for you.

1. "unlike safety testing, which is usually **mandatory**"

   a. optional   <u>b. obligatory</u>   c. official   d. complicated   e. expensive

2. "it enables a company to **verify** its own internal test data"

   a. question   b. repeat   c. doubt   d. confirm   e. revise

3. "there are a number of other very **sound** business reasons"

   a. reliable   b. obvious   c. familiar   d. popular   e. modern

4. "one of the best ways to gain a demonstrable competitive **edge**"

   a. profit   b. price   c. advantage   d. product   e. guarantee

5. "performance tests also help a company to **secure** valuable approval and endorsements"

   a. promise   b. buy   c. sell   d. obtain   e. invent

6. "it can show to **retailers** that its products are the best in their class"

   a. competitors   b. sellers   c. investors   d. employees   e. individuals

d Complete the text with the correct past participles of the verbs in the box.

apply	base	compare	design	list	make	run	weigh

Comparative testing (like in the tests (1) _____*run*_____ and published by consumer magazines) is effective in determining which of several similar products or services are best for their intended function. Tests can be technical and objective, practical and subjective, or in the form of a head-to-head comparison between two or more products. Things like ease of use, dependability, and durability are (2) _____. Comparative testing is (3) _____ on unique goals and objectives and, most often, tests are (4) _____ to suit the product or service and its application. When designing a comparative test, first all the features that are important to the end user are (5) _____. Following the tests, scores are (6) _____ to all the features to arrive at an overall score. Then, this score is (7) _____ against the initial cost to determine a "value for money" rating. With this information, recommendations are (8) _____ as regards product enhancements or the product's conditions for use.

e Read the following comparative test program and, in pairs, answer the questions.

- A review of the manufacturer's claims regarding features and performance.
- Energy consumption tests at varying ambient temperatures and with varying loads.
- Tests to verify temperature accuracy and stability at varying temperatures and with varying loads.
- Thermal tests to determine the loads that can safely be frozen.
- Thermal tests to determine how long the appliance will stay cold when there is a power failure.
- User tests to determine ease of use.
- A listing and rating of the features that make the appliance easier or more difficult to use as compared with others.

1. What appliance is being tested?
2. What other tests could be carried out on this appliance?

f In groups, devise a series of tests to apply to one of the items in the box or to an item of your own choosing.

a microwave oven	a hairdryer	a camping stove	a lawn mower	a photocopier

Task:
Design a new household product

You work in the design department of a large manufacturing company that makes a wide variety of household products.

With your team:

1. Decide on a product for your design project.

2. Determine the following three characteristics of your product:

   - how quickly it has to be brought to market
   - whether it is to be a high-quality or a low-quality product
   - whether it is to be a high-cost or a low-cost product

3. Decide on the relative importance of various design criteria (convenience, durability, efficiency, beauty, safety, etc.) for your product.

4. Decide which, if any, value engineering principles can be applied to your design in order to optimize costs.

5. Decide what sort of performance testing will be carried out on your product before it is released.

6. Give a presentation of your finished design proposal complete with any relevant sketches, models, diagrams, graphs, charts, tables, etc.

Unit 3

Manufacturing and Industry

Expert knowledge in a variety of fields

a Discuss these questions in pairs or small groups.

1. What do industrial engineers do?
2. What areas of expertise are especially relevant to industrial engineering?
3. In what sorts of fields do industrial engineers work?

b Complete the sentences with the phrases. There is one extra phrase.

1. Industrial engineers manage the layout and the design of . . .   _____*f*_____
2. They try to achieve the most advantageous and efficient . . .   _____
3. They schedule and direct the placement and the flow of . . .   _____
4. They organize personnel and equipment and try to optimize . . .   _____
5. They supervise the running of the plant and ensure that . . .   _____

a. raw materials, components, and machine parts.
b. the use of human resources.
c. the whole operation runs safely.
d. workers and management.
e. deployment of the site and the machinery.
f. industrial and manufacturing facilities.

c Listen to check your answers.

CD
T-15

d In pairs or small groups, complete the list of the areas of expertise that you think are particularly relevant for an industrial engineer.

Industrial Engineering: areas of expertise
facility layout and design
machinery and equipment

e Listen to an industrial engineer and complete your notes. Check and compare your answers.

CD
T-16

f In pairs, discuss your answers and reactions to what you heard. Discuss the areas of expertise that industrial engineering has in common with your own field.

> *In my field, human resources are not so important, but materials and components play a large part.*

g Complete the text about the work and role of industrial engineers with nouns from the box. There are two extra nouns.

efficiency	elements	facilities	firms	industries	management
	profitability	question	resources	safety	

Industrial engineers can work almost anywhere. Some work in places like car manufacturing plants or food processing plants while others work in health care (1) ____*facilities*____. Some work for management consulting (2) _____ while others work for organizations such as banks.

Industrial engineers are concerned with management, in the broadest sense of the word. Their role is to help (3) _____ to improve their efficiency, their effectiveness, their productivity, and their (4) _____. They help companies to stay competitive in the market. I see their job in terms of three key points: there is the question of (5) _____ — the most advantageous deployment of all (6) _____; there is the (7) _____ of cost—the economics of production; and there is the very important issue of human safety and well-being. These three key (8) _____ have to be balanced carefully.

h Reread the completed text and answer the questions.

1. How would industrial engineering in an auto plant differ from that in a food processing plant?

_____

2. What industrial engineering skills would be required by a banking organization?

_____

3. What could be the risks of giving too much importance to questions of efficiency?

_____

4. What could happen if a company implemented excessively rigorous safety measures?

_____

i Reread the discussion questions at the start of the lesson and then discuss these questions in pairs or small groups.

1. What new insights have you gained about industrial engineering?

2. What else have you learned about industrial engineering from this lesson?

3. What aspects of industrial engineering do you find most and least appealing?

Lesson 2
Working for an electric utility company

a Read and complete the text with the correct form of the verbs in the box or with other words (nouns, adjectives, etc.) derived from these verbs. Use each of the verbs in the box twice.

branch	diversify	employ	generate	invent	produce

Electrical Engineering is the largest and most (1) _____ field of engineering and is the discipline that (2) _____ the largest number of engineers. It involves the development, design, application, and manufacture of systems and devices that (3) _____ and use electric power and electric signals. Despite its great (4) _____, electrical engineering can be divided into four main (5) _____: electric power, communications, electronics, and computer hardware. Electrical engineering first developed with the (6) _____, distribution, and utilization of electric power. Electrical engineers design and manufacture (7) _____, motors, transmission systems, and controls. When the vacuum tube was (8) _____, electrical engineering (9) _____ into communications systems, including radio and television, and electronic engineering. Later, with the (10) _____ of the transistor, electrical and computer engineers were (11) _____ to (12) _____ the hardware needed for storing, processing, and transferring information.

 b Listen to four electrical engineers and write the number of each speaker in the correct column.

CD
T-17

electric power	communications	electronics	computer hardware

History capsule

Two key inventions in the history of electrical engineering were the transistor, invented by engineers at Bell Labs in 1947, and the integrated circuit (commonly known as the silicon chip), developed at Texas Instruments in 1959.

c Now read about four more electrical engineers and underline the correct verb form in each sentence.

1. I (<u>work</u> / am working) for a company that produces radar and navigation systems for ships. We (are doing / do) a lot of work for the Navy. _____

2. This company (makes / is making) components for the automobile industry. Right now, I (am working / work) on a device that monitors engine functions. _____

3. I (design / am designing) monitors. I (am creating / create) a new, cheaper flat-screen monitor. _____

4. I (work / am working) for an electric utility company. I (am operating / operate) the transmission devices at the power station. _____

 d Listen to check your answers.

CD
T-18

e Read the sentences in Exercise **c** again and label each one with the correct heading from the chart in Exercise **b**.

 f In pairs, discuss the questions.

1. Which speakers in Exercise **c** focus on what they habitually do?
2. Which speakers talk about their current activities?

g Write four sentences, two in the simple present and two in the present continuous, about your field of study or work.

1. _____
2. _____
3. _____
4. _____

h Write about your own field or any field other than electrical engineering. Include information about each of the topics in the box.

- general definitions and terms
- a brief history of the field
- things that are manufactured in this field
- areas of knowledge that people are required to master
- activities that people typically carry out

Lesson 3
Coordinating their computer systems

a Complete the notes with information that is true for your country.

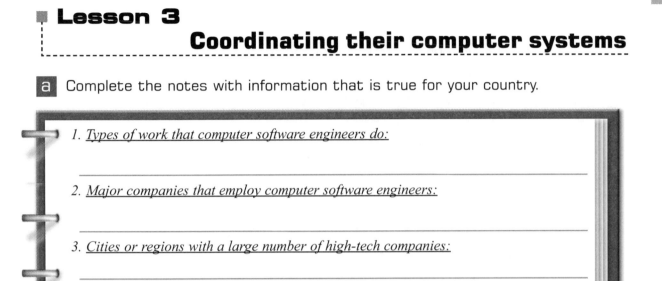

1. _Types of work that computer software engineers do:_

   _____

2. _Major companies that employ computer software engineers:_

   _____

3. _Cities or regions with a large number of high-tech companies:_

   _____

b Discuss your answers in pairs or small groups.

c Read the interview and write the questions that you think the interviewer asked.

Claudia Ramos,
software engineer

This week's "Meet the Engineer" features Claudia Ramos, who works at SysTech's San Francisco office.

Q: 1. _____
A: I'm a computer systems software engineer.

Q: 2. _____
A: I coordinate the construction and maintenance of a company's computer systems.

Q: 3. _____
A: A bit of both. I'm here some of the time but I also spend a lot of time on site configuring and installing computer systems at a company.

Q: 4. _____
A: Well, companies have various needs. They have to organize things like ordering, inventory, billing, payroll, etc. I help companies to coordinate their computer systems in these departments.

Q: 5. _____
A: No, not really. As a software engineer, I need to have good programming skills, but I'm more concerned with developing algorithms and analyzing and solving programming problems than with actually writing code programs.

Q: 6. _____
A: I also help companies to set up their intranet systems and, in general, I make suggestions about the technical direction of a company and I help them to plan for future growth.

d Listen to check and compare your answers.

CD
T-19

e Practice the interview in pairs.

f In pairs, discuss these questions about the interview.

1. What verb tense does Claudia use when describing her job?
   Why does she use this tense?
2. What verb tense does she use to talk about unchanging facts about companies?
   Why does she use this tense?

g Write the numbers of the sentences in the correct columns in the chart. The first one has been done for you.

1. Claudia likes working for SysTech.
2. Claudia usually drives to work.
3. Many companies use an intranet.
4. Claudia wants to start her own company one day.
5. Software engineers solve technical problems.
6. Claudia checks her e-mail every day.
7. Claudia doesn't work on Sundays.
8. Claudia enjoys her job.
9. Claudia has good programming skills.
10. Claudia hardly ever has time for lunch.

Principal uses of the simple present tense		
habitual or repeated actions, routines	general timeless statements or eternal truths about the world	relatively fixed attitudes, feelings, opinions
		1,

h Write two more sample sentences of your own for each category in the chart.

i In pairs, take turns describing what you or a member of your family do/does for a living. Use the *simple present* tense.

> *I work for a software company.*

> *My brother designs turbines.*

j In groups of four, exchange information about what people do.

k In your notebook, write a thirty-word description of what you do or a member of your family does for a living.

Lesson 4
Describing chemical engineering tasks

a Look at the illustrations and answer the questions in pairs.

1. What chemical processes are represented here?
2. What products can be manufactured using these chemical processes?

b Read and complete the text with the connecting words and phrases from the box. There are two extra items.

and	because	but	due
either	since	neither	that
is	thus		

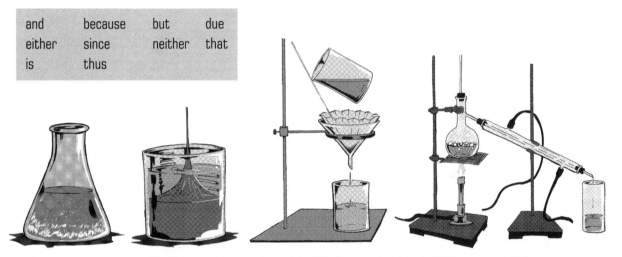

Chemical engineering is the application of chemistry—especially chemical reactions—to the process of converting (1) _____*either*_____ raw materials or chemical substances into more useful or valuable forms. Chemical engineers design, construct, and operate industrial equipment (2) _____ they devise chemical processes that can be used to produce chemical products on a large, (3) _____, an industrial scale. (4) _____ of the diversity of the materials dealt with in industry, individual chemical engineering tasks are described in terms of unit processes. (5) _____, chemical engineers working in these areas are process engineers. (6) _____ to technological advances, the number of unit processes has increased, (7) _____ the following continue to be important: distillation, crystallization, dissolution, filtration, extraction, and polymerization.

c Listen to the chemical engineer and number the topics in the order they are mentioned. Then listen again and complete the sentences on Page 37.

CD T-20

cost	initial challenge	processes and equipment	sequence	theoretical knowledge
_____	_____	_____	_____	_____

1. The chemical engineer mentions two laws: _____
2. The chemical engineer has to select and specify _____
3. What this chemical engineer found challenging was _____

d Combine these three sentences into one single sentence.

Continuous or assembly-line operations are more efficient and economical than batch processes.
Continuous or assembly-line operations lend themselves to automatic control.
Chemical engineers were among the first to incorporate automatic controls into their designs.

_____
_____
_____

CD
T-21

e Listen to check your answer.

f Match each chemical process with its layperson definition.

1. crystallization	_b_	a.	using a filter to separate a mixture mechanically
2. dissolution	___	b.	forming solid crystals from a homogenous solution
3. distillation	___	c.	separating substances based on differences in their vapor pressures
4. filtration	___	d.	dissolving a substance into a liquid
5. polymerization	___	e.	separating the compounds of a mixture based on the difference in solubility of a compound in various solvents
6. solvent extraction	___	f.	combining simple molecules to form more complex molecules of higher molecular weight and with different physical properties

g Choose two of the terms from the box and write definitions for them that could be understood by a layperson.

evaporation	absorption	humidification	adsorption

1. _____
2. _____

h In pairs, role-play conversations in which a chemical engineer explains some of the processes in Exercises **g** and **h** to a layperson.

i Choose two of the products from the box and write a report about how they are produced and which chemical principles and processes are involved in their manufacture.

synthetic fibers for clothing	soaps and detergents	paints

Lesson 5
Combining semiconductors with phosphors

a In pairs, discuss the questions.

1. What do the letters LED stand for?
2. What do you know about LEDs?
3. When and where were they invented?
4. What sorts of devices use LEDs?

b Complete the spaces in the text with *is* or *are* plus one of the prepositions in the box. The first two have been done for you.

as	by (x 3)	from	in (x 2)	through	with

An LED (light-emitting diode) is a device that emits visible light when an electric current passes through it. To manufacture LEDs, semiconductors (1) ___are___ combined (2) ___with___ phosphors. When electricity (3) _____ passed (4) _____ a diode, infrared radiation (5) _____ emitted (6) _____ the semiconductor. This radiation (7) _____ absorbed (8) _____ the phosphors in the diode and it (9) _____ then reemitted (10) _____ visible light. LEDs (11) _____ used (12) _____ the indicator lights and in the alphanumeric displays on many of the electronic devices and appliances that we use at home and at work.

The semiconductors that (13) _____ used (14) _____ LEDs are called III-V compound semiconductors. This is because they (15) _____ made (16) _____ combinations of elements from column III of the periodic table (aluminum, gallium, and indium) and elements from column V of the periodic table (phosphorus, arsenic, and antimony). The precise ratio of column III elements to column V elements in a semiconductor (17) _____ selected (18) _____ the manufacturer. In this way, the specific characteristics of an LED—color, the amount of visible versus infrared radiation, and brightness —are determined.

History capsule

The Periodic Table of Elements, which orders the elements according to their atomic numbers and groups them in columns according to shared chemical characteristics, was devised in 1869 by Russian chemist Dmitri Mendeleyev (1834–1907).

c Read the completed text in Exercise **b** and match the two halves of the sentences.

1. LEDs are made from semiconductors and . . . ___*c*___   a. compound semiconductors.
2. The phosphors turn infrared radiation into . . . _____   b. elements can be adjusted.
3. LEDs are used in the alphanumeric displays on . . . _____   c. phosphors.
4. LED semiconductors are known as III-V . . . _____   d. brightness of an LED.
5. The ratio of column III and column V . . . _____   e. electronic devices.
6. The ratio of III and V elements affects the . . . _____   f. visible light.

d Check ✓ the types of texts where the passive voice is more likely to be used.

☐ a newspaper report   ☐ a public notice

☐ a personal letter   ☐ a description of a technical process

☐ a set of instructions   ☐ a postcard

☐ an article in a scientific journal   ☐ an entry in a personal diary

☐ a children's story   ☐ a company press release

e In pairs, compare and discuss the types of passive voice texts that you come across in your own field of study or work.

I often have to read sets of instructions.

f In your notebook, write a description of a technical, industrial, or manufacturing process using the *passive voice* in the present. Use the verb participles in the box plus any other verbs you know.

Example:

The metal is heated. The components are assembled. The metal parts are then attached to the base.

assembled	cleaned	connected
constructed	converted	evaluated
extracted	heated	inserted
joined	manufactured	measured
placed	processed	programmed
removed	selected	separated
studied	tested	treated

g In small groups, take turns reading aloud descriptions of manufacturing or technical processes without saying the name of the final product. Your classmates have to guess what is being described.

Lesson 6
Mechanical engineers also design tools

CD
T-22

a Listen to four people talking about mechanical engineering and identify the main topic of each conversation. Choose from the topics in the box, and write the number of the topic next to the speaker in the chart below. Then listen again and complete each phrase below with the correct word.

1. what mechanical engineers make
2. how mechanical engineering developed
3. disciplines related to mechanical engineering
4. the nature of the work
5. opportunities in mechanical engineering
6. ideal qualities in a mechanical engineer
7. fundamental subjects of mechanical engineering

Speaker #1:	
Speaker #2:	
Speaker #3:	
Speaker #4:	

1. heat ___*transfer*___
2. refrigeration _____
3. theoretical _____
4. fluid _____
5. aerospace _____
6. electric _____

b Complete the following phrases with the preposition *of*, *in*, or *with*.

1. to be acquainted ____*with*____
2. to be aware _____
3. to be conversant _____
4. to be expert _____
5. to be familiar _____
6. to be proficient _____
7. to be well-versed _____
8. to have some knowledge _____

c In pairs, discuss the meaning of each phrase. Then sort the phrases in Exercise **b** and those in the box below into two general groups: (1) those phrases that express a high level of knowledge and (2) those that express a lesser degree of knowledge. Arrange them into two columns in your notebooks.

to have the know-how	to know backwards	to know your stuff	to master
	to know something like the back of your hand		to know the basics

d Write sentences in your notebook about your own level of knowledge and expertise in specific areas of your field of study or work. Then compare and discuss your sentences with a classmate.

I am completely conversant with . . .
I know the basics of . . .

e In pairs, role-play a conversation with an engineer or a scientist from a field other than mechanical engineering. Use the four questions from the listening material in Exercise **a** as the basis for your role play.

f Choose one of the three topics in Exercise **a** that are not mentioned in the interviews. Research the topic and present an oral report for the rest of the class.

g In pairs or small groups, discuss the questions.

1. What role do computers play in your particular field of study or work?
2. What specific tasks are you required to perform using some sort of computer?
3. How were these tasks performed before computers existed?

h Read the text and match each underlined verb with the most appropriate less formal synonym. Use the infinitive form of the verb.

Computers <u>assist</u> mechanical engineers by <u>performing</u> accurate and efficient computation, and by <u>permitting</u> the modeling and simulation of a new design as well as <u>facilitating</u> changes to an existing design. Computer-Aided Design (CAD) and Computer-Aided Manufacturing (CAM) are <u>employed</u> for design data processing and for <u>converting</u> a design into a product.

1. allow	*permit*		4. help	_____
2. carry out	_____		5. make easier	_____
3. change	_____		6. use	_____

i In pairs, role-play a conversation in which a mechanical engineer, or an engineer or scientist from another field, explains a technical process or operation in simplified terms to a layperson.

Task:
Plan a new manufacturing facility

You are an industrial engineer. You have been asked to prepare a proposal regarding the setting up of a completely new manufacturing facility.

With your team:

1. Decide what sort of products are to be manufactured at the new plant.

2. Plan the layout and the design of the site for the new plant.

3. Determine the most advantageous and efficient deployment of the machinery you are going to use.

4. Determine the placement and the flow of the raw materials, components, and machine parts that will be brought into the plant.

5. Draw up lists of the personnel that will be required to run the plant efficiently and write brief job descriptions for different categories of workers.

6. Outline any special safety issues or procedures that are relevant to the work to be carried out at the plant.

7. Present your finished proposal complete with any relevant sketches, scale models, diagrams, graphs, charts, tables, etc.

Unit 4

Safety, Maintenance, and Quality Control

What caused the explosion

a Look at the photograph and, in pairs, answer the questions.

1. What accident does the photograph show?
2. When and where did this incident take place?
3. What caused the accident?
4. How many lives were lost in the accident?

b Skim through the text quickly to check your answers.

A NASA space shuttle consists of three major components: a winged orbiter that carries both crew and cargo, an external tank containing liquid hydrogen (fuel) and liquid oxygen (oxidizer) for the orbiter's three main rocket engines, and a pair of large solid-propellant rocket boosters (SRBs).

On January 28, 1986, the Challenger shuttle and its crew of seven (including teacher Christa McAuliffe, who had been selected to be the first private citizen in space) were destroyed shortly after launch from Cape Canaveral, Florida. The primary cause of the loss of the *Challenger* was the failure of an O-ring seal of a joint on one of the solid rocket boosters.

The SRBs are constructed in four cylindrical sections. These have to be sealed together completely to prevent the escape of the extremely hot by-products of the burning fuel during a launch. The O-rings are rubber rings that play a vital part in sealing the joints.

On the day of the launch, the weather was unusually cold and this caused the rubber of one of the O-rings on the joint between the bottom two segments of the right SRB to become brittle. This, combined with the faulty design of the joint, allowed hot gases from the burning solid rocket fuel to escape. The gases and flames burned through the metal that held the SRB in position. When the SRB broke off, it ruptured the side of the external fuel tank. This allowed the liquid hydrogen and oxygen to mix prematurely and this is what caused the explosion.

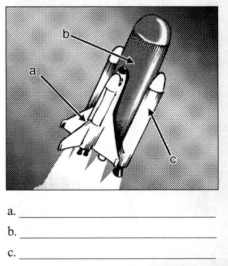

a. _____

b. _____

c. _____

c Read the first paragraph of the text and, in the diagram, label the three main components of the space shuttle.

History capsule

Another tragic accident occurred on February 1, 2003, when the *Columbia* space shuttle broke up over north-central Texas at an altitude of about 40 miles (60 kilometers) as it was returning from an orbital mission. All seven crew members died in the accident.

d Read through the text again and complete the sentences with *because* or *so*.

1. The O-ring was brittle _____ the weather was cold.
2. The O-ring was brittle, _____ this allowed hot gases to escape from the SRB.
3. The metal holding the rocket was damaged, _____ the rocket broke loose.
4. The hydrogen and oxygen mixed and exploded _____ the rocket ruptured the fuel tank.

e In your notebook, write four conditional sentences about the causes of the accident.

If the weather had not been cold, the O-ring would not have become brittle.

f Draw a series of diagrams to explain exactly what caused the *Challenger* accident.

g In pairs or small groups, discuss your reactions to what you read in the text.

h Listen to an interview with a NASA spokesperson and answer the questions.

CD
T-23
1. When was the Presidential Commission on the Space Shuttle *Challenger* Accident created?
2. Who was named chairman of the commission?
3. Who set up the *Challenger* Data and Design Analysis Task Force?
4. How long did the commission's investigation take?
5. How many people were involved in the investigation?
6. When was the commission's report published?

i Listen to the next part of the interview and complete the notes.

CD
T-24

1. SRBs:

2. A new joint design:

3. Main space shuttle engines:

4. Office of Safety, Reliability, Maintainability, and Quality Assurance:

j Research and prepare a report about another accident. Describe what caused the accident (mechanical failure, electrical failure, materials failure, human error, etc.), how the accident could have been avoided, and what happened as a consequence of the accident.

Lesson 2

The prevention of accidents

a Look at the four types of engineers and, in pairs, discuss the questions.

| safety engineer | operating engineer | maintenance engineer | control engineer |

1. What differences are there between these types of engineers?
2. What do these fields of engineering have in common?

b Listen to check and compare your answers.

CD
T-25

c Read the interview and write the questions that you think the interviewer asked.

Q: 1. _____?
A: Many large industrial and construction firms employ safety
   engineers. Also nowadays, insurance companies working
   in the field of employee compensation maintain safety
   engineering departments.

Q: 2. _____?
A: In most cases, safety engineering is a specialty adopted
   by engineers who received their initial training in some
   other branch of engineering.

Q: 3. _____?
A: Well, the principal objective of engineers working in this
   field is preventing accidents. Safety engineers work on
   ways of safeguarding all types of worker but particularly the ones who work in occupations that
   can be hazardous.

Q: 4. _____?
A: No, not all of them. You see, some safety engineers also help in the design of machinery, factories,
   ships, and roads. They suggest modifications and improvements to try to reduce the likelihood of
   an accident.

d Match each word from the interview with the correct definition.

1. compensation   _e_   a. protect
2. initial   _____   b. small, specific change to something
3. safeguard   _____   c. probability, chance
4. hazardous   _____   d. existing at the beginning
5. modification   _____   e. payment for damage, harm, or loss
6. likelihood   _____   f. dangerous, risky

e Read through the text and, for each phrasal verb in parentheses, suggest a more formal replacement from the box, in the correct form. There are four extra verbs.

conceal	eliminate	ensure	initiate	maintain
modify	prevent	propose	reduce	seek

As we have seen, safety engineers can offer help at the design stage by (1) ___*proposing*___ (put forward) improvements that can (2) _____ (cut down) the risk of accidents. For example, when some new machinery is being designed, a safety engineer tries to find ways to (3) _____ (get rid of) any dangerous projecting parts that might hurt someone. The safety engineer tries to (4) _____ (cover up) the moving parts of a machine to minimize the chance of accidental contact with the operator. The safety engineer will also (5) _____ (make sure) that any emergency cutoff switches are within reach of the operator.

As for the design of safer roads, when a new road system is being designed, safety engineers (6) _____ (look for) ways of avoiding hazards like sharp turns or blind intersections—things that have been known to cause traffic accidents.

f Write a list of adjectives that describe the personal and professional qualities that you think are required in the field of safety engineering.

responsible, thorough, methodical, . . .

g In pairs, compare and discuss your ideas. Then discuss with other pairs the personal and professional qualities that are required in your particular field of study or work.

In my field, you need a lot of patience and you have to be able to concentrate.

h In small groups, conduct a physical inspection of your school or place of work and fill out a chart like the one below.

location	potential danger	recommendation for improvement

i Write an account of an accident that you or someone you know had at school or work. Describe what happened, what caused the accident, and how, if at all, it could have been avoided.

Wearing special clothes

a Look at the photograph and, in pairs, discuss the questions.

1. What do you observe in the photograph?

2. What sort of work do you think is being carried out here?

3. Why do you think the people are wearing special clothing?

CD
T-26

b Listen to the speakers and complete the notes with the correct information. Then listen again and circle the statements *True* or *False*.

Name: Stephanie
Occupation:
Current job/project:

Name: Greg
Occupation:
Current job/project:

Name: Carol
Occupation:
Current job/project:

Name: Tomas
Occupation:
Current job/project:

1. Stephanie has to wear a special vest when working at night.	True	False
2. Greg never has to work behind a protective screen.	True	False
3. Carol has to wear special clothes at work all the time.	True	False
4. Tomas must wear a hard hat at work.	True	False
5. Tomas can wear a tie if he wants to.	True	False

c Give examples of the following concepts

1. Something that is prohibited   _____
2. Something that is obligatory   _____
3. Something that is not obligatory   _____
4. Something that is permitted   _____

d Match the expressions with the concepts.

1. allowed to   _____   a. this is prohibited
2. must   _____   b. this is obligatory
3. mustn't   _____   c. this is not obligatory
4. don't have to   _____   d. this is permitted

e Complete the sentences with an appropriate expression. Use *must, mustn't, have to*, or *don't/doesn't have to.*

1. Our boss is very strict about punctuality. We _____ arrive on time.
2. The dress code here is quite informal. For example, men _____ wear a tie.
3. You _____ eat or drink near the computers. This is forbidden.
4. This is a smoke-free area. If you want to smoke, you _____ go outside.
5. You _____ eat in the canteen, but you can if you like.
6. One piece of advice—you _____ park in the boss's parking space!

f In small groups, discuss the rules that people have to follow in your school or place of work. Use the suggestions in the box plus your own ideas.

Do you have to wear formal clothes to work?

safety rules	safety equipment	dress code	punctuality
eating and drinking	smoking	ways of addressing people	

g In your notebook, write three sentences about rules at your school or place of work. Write two statements that are true and one that is false.

I have to arrive at work at eight o'clock. Men don't have to wear suits.

h Take turns reading aloud your statements from Exercise **g** and have your classmates guess which statement is the false one.

The amplitude of motion

a Look at the photographs and, in pairs, discuss the questions.

1. What is happening in the photographs?
2. What happened to this bridge?
3. What do you think was the cause of the problem?

b Listen to check your answers. Complete the notes.

CD
T-27

Tacoma Narrows Bridge
  1. Year of construction:

  _____

  2. Location:
  _____

  3. Number of months in operation:
  _____

  4. Length of span:
  _____

  _____

c Using models, drawings, or any other visual aid, demonstrate the following three different types of movement that the Tacoma Narrows Bridge exhibited before it collapsed.

1. The bridge buckles along its whole length.
2. The bridge twists with one side going down as the other side lifts up.
3. The midpoint of the bridge stays still while the two halves of the bridge twist in opposite directions.

d Complete the text using the words below.

criteria
vibrate
load
stresses
comply
limit
methodology

Limit state design is a design (1) _methodology_ used by structural and civil engineers. Structures and buildings are usually designed to (2) _____ with codes that are based on limit state theory. A limit state is a set of performance (3) _____ covering, for example, strength, tendency to (4) _____, stability, tendency to buckle or twist, etc. These are the criteria that must be met when a structure is subjected to various types of (5) _____. A structure or a building has to satisfy two main criteria: the ultimate limit state (ULS) and the serviceability limit state (SLS). To satisfy ULS criteria, all the types of (6) _____ (bending, shearing, compression, etc.) that a particular element (a column or a beam, for example) could be subjected to must be below an established (7) _____.

e Using a dictionary, write a definition for each of the following verbs in the context of structural movement and damage.

1. bend: _____
2. buckle: _____
3. twist: _____
4. shear: _____

f Read the interview and then discuss the questions in pairs or small groups.

Q: You mentioned two main criteria: the ultimate limit state and the serviceability limit state. Tell us more about the serviceability limit state.

A: Well, the purpose of SLS requirements is to make sure that people inside a structure are not upset or alarmed by large deflections or vibrations in the floor when they walk. SLS criteria also require the beam deflections in a roof to be low enough to ensure that the plaster or the paint on the ceiling does not crack or fall off. SLS requirements limit the excessive swaying from side to side of a building or of a bridge in high winds—something that might make people feel sick.

Q: So, are SLS requirements less stringent than ULS criteria?

A: Yes, they are. A structure that may fail to satisfy certain SLS criteria is not necessarily unsafe or likely to fall down!

1. Have you ever been inside a building that made you feel physically unsafe in some way?
2. What characteristics of a building or a structure might make a person feel nervous or uneasy?
3. What other aspects of a building or a structure do you think should be covered by SLS criteria?

g In groups, look for information about the standards, codes, and specifications that govern structural engineering and civil engineering projects in your country. Present your findings in an oral report.

h You have been asked to carry out an inspection of a bridge, a tower, or some other public building to check that it is structurally sound. In small groups, discuss what aspects of the structure you will examine, what measurements you will take, what tests you will apply, etc.

i Find out about the regulations governing the construction of the building(s) that you study or work in and present your findings in a report.

The design of this building has to comply with standards established by the Department of . . .

Lesson 5

Quality and a finished item

a In pairs or small groups, discuss the questions.

1. What do you understand by the concept of "quality"?
2. What is it that marks some products as high-quality and others as low-quality?
3. What products have you bought that exhibited poor quality? What exactly was wrong with them?

b Read the text and number the paragraphs in the correct order.

The introduction of mass production and piecework in the early twentieth century brought benefits, but, ironically, also created problems with quality. With piecework, workers could earn more money by producing more products. This led to some poor workmanship being passed on to the assembly lines. To address this problem, full-time inspectors started to be introduced into large-scale factories during the 1920s and 1930s.

SPC provides inspectors with a sampling system. As opposed to a 100% inspection, which is costly and time-consuming, traditional SPC usually involves random sampling and testing of a fraction of total output. Any variances from established levels of tolerance are continuously tracked and, thus, manufacturing processes are corrected to prevent defective parts from being produced.

In manufacturing, the role of quality control and quality engineering is to develop systems to ensure that products are designed and produced to meet or exceed customers' requirements and expectations. These systems are often set up in conjunction with other business and engineering disciplines using a cross-functional approach.

Companies, mainly in the USA, adopted a systematic approach to quality control during the 1930s. Gradually, they saw the need to introduce a more rigorous type of quality control. This came to be known as statistical process control (SPC). This system was born of the realization that quality cannot be inspected into a finished item. So, instead of just inspecting finished items, the inspection phase was extended backwards.

c Read the text again and answer the questions.

1. Which other business and engineering disciplines do you think would be involved in a quality control system?
   _____

2. What benefits do you think the introduction of mass production brought to companies?
   _____

3. Why would the introduction of piecework increase the chances of poor workmanship being passed on to an assembly line?
   _____

4. In what way was the inspection phase "extended backwards"?
   _____

5. Why do companies not inspect 100% of their output?
   _____

d Discuss the questions in pairs or small groups.

1. What sort of quality control systems or programs are in operation in your school or place of work?

2. What systems, methods, philosophies, etc., of quality control have you heard of? How do they work?

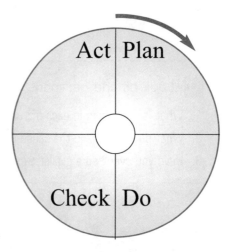

CD
T-28
e Listen to the interview about PDCA and, in the diagram, add your notes to the main steps of the cycle.

f Read and complete the text with the adverbs in the box.

approximately	inevitably	precisely	repeatedly	widely

The PDCA approach, also known as the Shewhart Cycle, is one of the most (1) _____ used quality control paradigms. Named for Walter A. Shewhart, it was made opular by Dr. W. Edwards Deming. To be effective, PDCA cycles should be implemented (2) _____ and each repetition should begin as soon as possible with each cycle taking you closer and closer toward your objective. The approach is based on the idea that people's knowledge and skills are, (3) _____, limited, but also capable of improvement over time. So, even though key information may be lacking, it is better to make some sort of start and to be (4) _____ right rather than (5) _____ wrong. Over time, and with improving knowledge and skills, a series of PDCA cycles can help people to define and achieve their objectives.

g Discuss the questions in pairs.

1. How valid and useful do you judge the PDCA approach to be?

2. In what areas of your studies or work could the PDCA approach be implemented?

3. What changes or refinements would you make to this approach to quality control?

h Look for information about other quality control systems and methods and prepare a written report.

History capsule

In the United Kingdom, some people use the phrase "a Friday car" to describe a new car that frequently breaks down or shows other defects in quality. The expression refers to cars manufactured on Fridays by workers who are thinking about the weekend, hurrying to finish for the day, and, thus, concentrating less on the quality of their work.

Lesson 6

A "total quality control" approach

a Look at the cartoons and, in pairs, discuss the questions.

1. What is happening in each picture?
2. What do you think is the cause of the problem?
3. Have you ever had a similar experience with an electrical appliance?

b Read and complete the text with the letters of the phrases in the box.

a. what the customer requires	b. into a finished product	c. sales keep on falling
d. shown in increased sales and profits		e. reliability, maintainability, and safety

Statistical quality control techniques usually produce positive results that are (1) _____. However, sometimes, despite the implementation of a quality control program, (2) _____. The most common reason for this is that the original product specifications do not sufficiently take into account the most important factor, i.e., (3) _____. Remember, if the original specifications do not reflect the correct quality requirements, it's no good trying to inspect or manufacture quality (4) _____. The three most common characteristics that tend to be neglected are (5) _____.

c Listen to check your answers.

CD
T-29

d Discuss these questions in pairs or small groups.

1. What do you understand by the term total quality control?
2. How do you think it differs from statistical quality control?

e Read this report by a quality engineer. Complete each space with a verb from the box.

being	expanding	implementing	listening	losing
	replacing	setting	using	

EZ-Kleen vacuum cleaner

The original product specifications for the *EZ-Kleen* vacuum cleaner do not reflect the correct quality requirements. Key factors like reliability, maintainability, and safety have been neglected and so sales have fallen. To avoid (1) _____*losing*_____ more sales, I suggest (2) _____ a "total quality control" approach by making changes in the following areas:

- Rather than keep on (3) _____ its outdated definitions of customer requirements, Marketing should obtain better, more up-to-date information.
- Product specifications should be redefined to conform to these requirements.
- Conformance to specifications should be ensured at every stage of manufacturing.
- Management should verify that all operators are equal to the work asked of them. The company should consider (4) _____ workers with a poor track record.
- Quality Control should carry out inspections and tests to ensure that all components and materials conform to the specifications. They should check all measuring equipment.
- The company should think about (5) _____ Customer Service and bear in mind that it is worth (6) _____ carefully to customer feedback.

This company is used to (7) _____ specifications about materials and dimensions. However, in total quality control, the parameters also cover operating, safety, environmental, reliability, and maintainability requirements. In the future, I envisage (8) _____ able to implement total quality control throughout this company.

f In pairs, discuss and evaluate the proposals made in the report and add any further recommendations that you would make.

> *The company should consider changing its . . .*

g In your notebook, write sentences using the following verbs plus other verbs in the gerund (–ing) form: *delay, go on, postpone, risk, resume.*

> *If we don't implement a quality control program, we risk losing . . .*

Task:
Devise a quality control program

You work for a Quality Control consultancy firm. You have been asked to devise and implement an entire quality control program for a manufacturing company.

With your team:

1. Decide what sort of products the company manufactures.

2. Determine a production sequence for the manufacture of your product or products.

3. Devise a system of statistical process control to inspect a certain percentage of the company's output.

4. Discuss the merits of introducing PDCA cycles or some other quality control paradigm.

5. Outline a total quality approach that could be applied to the company's activities.

6. Give a presentation of your finished quality control plan complete with any relevant diagrams, graphs, charts, tables, etc.

Unit 5

Careers and Employment

a Look at the photographs and discuss the questions in small groups.

1. What differences do you observe between the two photographs?

2. What changes in the engineering profession are represented in the two photographs?

CD
T-30
b Listen to an interview with an experienced engineer and number the topics in the order you hear them. Then listen again and take notes of the key ideas for each topic.

> ***Trends in Engineering***
>
> ☐ *an interdisciplinary approach*
> _____
>
> ☐ *human-factors engineering or ergonomics*
> _____
>
> ☐ *licensure*
> _____
>
> ☐ *time-study engineering*
> _____

c Answer these questions about the interview.

1. What is the difference between time-study engineering and human-factors engineering?

_____

2. What example does the engineer give of an application of human-factors engineering?

_____

3. What point does the engineer clarify regarding an interdisciplinary approach to engineering?

_____

4. What types of construction project require approval by a professionally licensed engineer?

_____

d In pairs or small groups, discuss changes and trends that you have observed in your field of study or work.

> *We have seen an increase in the use of software simulations.*

e Using language that a layperson can understand, write an article about changes that have occurred in your chosen field of study or work.

> *My profession has become more specialized.*
> *For example, . . .*

f Read and complete the text with the given verbs in the correct tense. Use the *simple present, the simple past, the present perfect,* or *the future* with *will.*

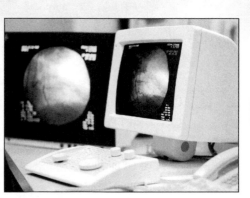

As in all areas of science and technology, computerization (1) _____ (play) an increasingly important role in engineering in recent years and this is something that (2) _____ (continue) in the future. Computers (3) _____ (help) engineers in many ways during the last thirty years or so.

Today, we (4) _____ (use) computers for solving complex problems as well as for handling, storing, and generating the vast quantity of data that we often (5) _____ (work) with. Also, CAD (computer-aided design) software (6) _____ (make) it easier for engineers to create drawings and models of their designs. In the past, we used to make prototypes, which (7) _____ (be) expensive and time-consuming. Now we (8) _____ (check) models for defects without always having to make a prototype.

g Discuss your answers in pairs and, in each instance, explain how you arrived at your answer.

h Read and discuss these predictions about the role of computers in science and engineering in the future.

1. In the future, computers will be able to think for themselves.
2. The increased use of computers will put most scientists and engineers out of work.
3. In the future, most scientists and engineers will work from home.
4. Future computers will all be solar-powered.

i Copy and complete the chart with ideas about your studies and work in the future.

A future event	When it will happen	How it will affect me	How I will need to deal with it

j Compare and discuss your ideas in pairs or small groups.

Lesson 2
Physicists and biotechnology firms

 a Look at the cartoon and, in pairs or small groups, discuss the questions.

1. What sort of scientist is depicted in this cartoon?

2. What stereotypical ideas about scientists are conveyed by the image?

3. What other stereotypical ideas exist about scientists and the world of science?

b Complete each sentence by matching the *if* clause with the appropriate general truth.

1. If you are working in the private sector, . . .   _d_

2. If you are an engineer, . . .   _____

3. If you are a physicist, . . .   _____

4. If you are a chemist, . . .   _____

5. If you have completed a degree in science or engineering, . . .   _____

6. If you want to do well in today's world, . . .   _____

a. you could be hired by a biotechnology firm.

b. you have proved that you can think analytically.

c. you might find yourself working for a pharmaceutical company.

d. you are coping with more stringent timeframes.

e. learn how to work in a team and how to communicate effectively.

f. you are probably working closer to an actual production line.

c Listen to check your answers.

CD
T-31

d Study these sentences and answer the questions.

If your field is biology, you could work in the biomedical field.

If you are looking for a bigger budget for your research project, make sure you have the communication skills necessary to argue your case.

If you have gotten this far, you have mastered a host of scientific theories and terminology.

1. What do you notice about the tenses of the verbs in each clause?

_____

2. How does the structure of these conditional sentences compare with other conditional forms you have studied?

_____

e Write definitions for the following phrases.

1. people-in-the-street _____

2. stringent timeframes _____

3. the purse strings _____

f Read and complete the text with the words in the box. There are two extra words.

analytical	enjoyable	financial	industrial	quantum
safety	stock	well-rounded	wide	

Getting a/an (1) _____ education is important because, either straight after college or after getting some experience in a science or engineering setting, you may want to change careers. For instance, if your field is biochemistry, you may eventually decide to work for a/an (2) _____ services institution as a biotech (3) _____ analyst. Increasingly, employers are realizing that the (4) _____ skills and computer experience that students acquire learning science and engineering can be put to use in a/an (5) _____ range of other professions like sales, marketing, and business consulting. If you have mastered (6) _____ physics, you probably treat something like stock market analysis as a/an (7) _____ break. And if you have good social skills and other interests outside of science, you may find it easier to make such a career change.

g Complete the sentences with information that is true for your field of study or work.

1. If you're interested in _____, then you should think about a career in _____.

2. If you've ever considered working as a _____, the best thing to study might be _____.

3. If your degree is in _____, you could find work in the field of _____.

h In pairs, role-play conversations about career options or career changes.

i Write a letter to a student offering advice and insight about career choices and opportunities, and possible career changes in the future.

History capsule

What do astronaut Neil Armstrong, former President Jimmy Carter, and movie director Alfred Hitchcock all have in common? They all started with an engineering education.

Lesson 3

Still a male-dominated profession

a Discuss the questions in pairs or small groups.

1. What is the ratio of women to men in your field of study or work?

2. How would you describe prevailing attitudes in your country regarding the entry of women into your field of study or work?

b Read the first paragraph of the text and fill in the blanks with your prediction of the percentage.

While women represent half of the population of the United States, they make up only (1) _____% of the country's physicists, just (2) _____% of its engineers, and only (3) _____% of its engineering students. Engineering is still a male-dominated profession, although women's participation in the engineering workforce has increased dramatically over the last (4) _____ years. Some engineering disciplines have a higher percentage of women professionals than others. For example, (5) _____% of chemical engineers, 11% of industrial engineers, (6) _____% of civil engineers, and 7% of electrical engineers are women.

c Listen to check your answers.

CD
T-32

d Read the next two paragraphs and discuss the questions in pairs.

As recently as 1975, women still earned fewer than 2.5% of all engineering degrees awarded in the United States. The number of women earning engineering degrees increased dramatically from the mid-1970s through the mid-1980s and then leveled off for the next ten years. The percentage of engineering degrees awarded to women continues to increase, but this is due in part to the declining number of men opting to study engineering.

More than 30% of bachelor's degrees in the fields of bio, environmental, chemical, industrial, and agricultural engineering are awarded to women and they earn 22.5% of bachelor's degrees in civil engineering. However, in the fields of electrical engineering and mechanical engineering, women receive respectively only 14% and 13.9% of the degrees awarded.

1. Why do you think there are more women in chemical engineering than in civil engineering?

2. How do you account for the difference between the numbers of women graduates and the numbers of women engineers?

3. Why do you think there are not so many women working in electrical engineering and mechanical engineering?

e Read part of an interview about women in science and engineering. Complete each phrasal verb with the correct particle (*up, off, away*, etc.).

Q: In your book, you point (1) ___*out*___ that many girls opt (2) _____ of math and science courses in middle school, and in this way they perhaps throw (3) _____ the chance of a career in science or engineering. Why is this?

A: I think one of the main reasons is that girls and young women pick (4) _____ discouraging messages—some subtle, some more direct—from adults, from their peers, and from the media, and these messages tend to put girls (5) _____.

Q: What sort of messages?

A: Well, people keep (6) _____ saying that, "Girls don't take (7) _____ technology." or "Boys are better at math and science than girls." or "A woman engineer can't be feminine."

f Now write a more formal equivalent for each phrasal verb.

(1) ___*point out = mention*_____

(2) _____   *(3)* _____

(4) _____   *(5)* _____

(6) _____   *(7)* _____

CD
T-33

g Listen to the rest of the interview and complete the notes.

A more diverse engineering community

1. Benefits for society in general:

   problem-solving: _____

   teamwork: _____

2. Benefits for business:

   customers' needs: _____

   design of products: _____

h In pairs, or small groups discuss the arguments put forward in the interview and how applicable they are to the situation in your country.

i Find out about a famous woman engineer and write an account of her life, her work, and her contributions to engineering. Choose one of the figures from the box if you wish.

Bette Nesmith Graham	Edith Flanigen	Ellen Ochoa	Grace Hopper
Maria Sklodowska	Martha Coston	Mary Walton	Patricia Billings
Patsy Sherman	Randi Altschul	Stephanie Louise Kwoleke	

Lesson 4
Many engineers are licensed PEs

 a Discuss the questions in pairs.

1. What is licensure?
2. What sort of professions require licensure in your country?

b Read the text and number the paragraphs in the correct order.

☐ New engineering graduates can start the licensing process by taking the examination in two stages. The initial Fundamentals of Engineering (FE) examination can be taken upon graduating.

|1| In the United States, engineers wishing to offer their services directly to the public have to be licensed. The title of Professional Engineer, or PE, is used for engineers who are licensed. Many civil, electrical, mechanical, and chemical engineers are licensed PEs.

☐ After having acquired relevant work experience, EITs can take the second examination, the Principles and Practice of Engineering.

☐ Generally, this licensure requires a degree from an engineering program accredited by the ABET (Accrediting Board for Engineering and Technology), four years of relevant work experience, and the successful completion of a State examination.

☐ Most states recognize licensure from other states as long as the way in which the initial license was obtained meets or exceeds their own licensure requirements. In several states, there are also mandatory continuing education requirements for relicensure.

☐ Engineers who pass this first examination are commonly referred to as Engineers in Training (EIT) or Engineer Interns (EI).

c Read the complete ordered text. Then read the statements and circle *True* or *False*.

1. The first engineering exams are called Fundamentals of Engineering.	True	False
2. By law, all engineers in the U.S. have to be licensed.	True	False
3. Engineers who pass the second stage of exams are known as EITs.	True	False
4. Licensed engineers are referred to as PEs.	True	False
5. To be licensed, engineers have to have four years of relevant experience.	True	False

d The register of the previous text is quite formal. In pairs, look carefully at the two sentences in the chart and discuss any differences between them.

formal register	*informal register*
The initial Fundamentals of Engineering (FE) examination can be taken upon graduating.	You can take the first exam—the FE—right after you graduate.

e Select two other sentences from the text and rewrite them in a more informal register.

1. _____

2. _____

f In pairs, role-play a conversation in which an expert explains licensure procedures, special terms, abbreviations, acronyms, etc., to a layperson or a non-expert.

Engineers who are licensed are called Professional Engineers, or PEs for short.

g In small groups, compare and discuss formal requirements in your own professional fields and discuss how you would explain these to a layperson.

h Complete the text with the correct abstract noun from the box.

development	independence	knowledge	management	supervision

New engineering graduates normally work under the (1) ___supervision___ of experienced engineers. In large companies, they may also receive formal classroom or seminar-type training. As they gain (2) _____ and experience, new engineers are assigned to more difficult projects and are given greater (3) _____ in design (4) _____, problem solving, and decision-making. Engineers may advance to become technical specialists or to supervise a staff or team of engineers and technicians. Some may eventually go into engineering (5) _____ or enter other managerial or sales fields.

i Using a dictionary to help you, make a list in your notebook of other words related to the ones highlighted in the previous exercise.

supervision (noun), supervise (verb), supervisor (noun)

j Using non-technical language, write about typical career paths that people in your chosen profession follow.

Lesson 5

Median annual earnings

a Complete the sentences about occupations with information that is true for your country.

1. In my country _____ earn more than _____.
2. Two of the highest earning professions are _____ and _____.
3. Among the lowest earning occupations are _____ and _____.
4. An engineer's average salary is about _____ a year.

b Discuss your answers in pairs or small groups.

c Look at the chart. Then read the statements and circle *True* or *False*.

Median annual earnings of different branches of engineering, 2002			
aerospace	$72,750	environmental	$61,410
agricultural	$50,700	materials	$62,590
biomedical	$60,410	mechanical	$62,880
chemical	$72,490	mining and geological	$61,770
civil	$60,070	nuclear	$81,350
computer hardware	$72,150	petroleum	$83,370

Source: Occupational Outlook Handbook, Bureau of Labor Statistics, U.S. Department of Labor

1. On average, biomedical engineers earn slightly more than civil engineers.	True	False
2. Of all the branches in the chart, agricultural engineers earn the least.	True	False
3. Environmental engineers earn a lot more than nuclear engineers.	True	False
4. Aerospace engineers and chemical engineers earn about the same amount.	True	False
5. Materials engineers earn slightly more than mechanical engineers.	True	False

d Correct the false statements in your notebook.

e In pairs, use the information in the chart to make sentences comparing different branches of engineering.

f In groups, discuss your reactions to the information in the chart. Try to account for differences in the average annual earnings of different branches of engineering.

g Listen and complete the text with the correct numbers and dates.

CD
T-34

Median annual earnings of aerospace engineers in 2002 were $72,750. The middle 50 percent earned between (1) ___$59,520___ and (2) _____. The lowest 10 percent earned less than $49,640, and the highest (3) _____ percent earned more than (4) _____.

According to a (5) _____ salary survey by the National Association of Colleges and Employers, bachelor's degree candidates in aerospace engineering received starting salary offers averaging (6) _____ a year, master's degree candidates were offered (7) _____, and Ph.D. candidates were offered $68,406.

Source: Occupational Outlook Handbook, Bureau of Labor Statistics, U.S. Department of Labor

h In pairs, practice reading aloud information from the following text.

Median annual earnings of mechanical engineers were $62,880 in 2002. The middle 50 percent earned between $50,800 and $78,040. The lowest 10 percent earned less than $41,490, and the highest 10 percent earned more than $93,430.

According to a salary survey conducted in 2003 by the National Association of Colleges and Employers, bachelor's degree candidates in mechanical engineering received starting offers averaging $48,585 a year, master's degree candidates had offers averaging $54,565, and Ph.D. candidates were initially offered $69,904.

Source: Occupational Outlook Handbook, Bureau of Labor Statistics, U.S. Department of Labor

i Look for information about average earnings in different branches of engineering in your country and prepare a brief written report like the ones on this page.

Lesson 6
Seeing an increase in opportunities

a Discuss the questions in pairs or small groups.

1. What is the overall career outlook for recent graduates in your field?

2. What factors influence or will influence the availability of jobs in your field?

b Skim through the text and choose the best heading for each section from the box below.

foreign influence	new technologies	natural wastage	overall outlook	layoffs

a. _____

As for the career outlook for engineering over the next ten years or so, well, I don't (1) _____
to have all the answers. I (2) _____ to see an increase in opportunities but this
will be slower than in other occupations. Why? Because many engineers (3) _____
to work in slow-growing manufacturing industries and this can hold down their employment growth. However, overall
job opportunities in engineering should be quite good because graduate numbers (4) _____
to be in balance with the number of jobs that will be available.

appear	claim	expect	tend

b. _____

Companies are aware of competitive pressures and advancing technology and they know that they (5) _____
to improve and update their products and optimize manufacturing processes. New computer and communications
systems have improved the design process and (6) _____ to continue doing so. Some people insist that
computer technologies (7) _____ to limit employment opportunities. Personally, I (8) _____ to
accept this point of view.

refuse	threaten	need	promise

c Now read and complete each paragraph with the verbs in each corresponding box.

d Listen to check your answers.

e Read the statements and underline the ones that are false.

1. Job growth in engineering will progress at the same rate as in other occupations.

2. The number of engineering graduates will be about the same as the number of job openings.

3. Computer and communications systems will continue to improve the design process in the future.

4. This engineer believes that computer technologies threaten to limit employment opportunities.

f Correct the false statements.

g Read the sentences and, in pairs, discuss to what extent they are true for your country and also to what extent they are true for your own field.

1. There are large numbers of well-trained, English-speaking engineers who agree to work at much lower salaries than engineers in the United States.

2. The trend in many firms toward contracting out engineering work to engineering services firms, either domestic or foreign, threatens to cause significant layoffs of engineers.

3. Much work previously done by engineers in the U.S.A. is now done by engineers in other countries. The rise of the Internet and other communications systems has helped to make this possible.

h Complete the text with words related to the words in the box. The first one has been done for you.

assessment	continuous	delivery	know
obsolete	promote	special	valuable

Engineers need to continue their education throughout their careers because much of their (1) _value_ to an employer depends on their (2) _____ of the latest technology. Though the pace of change varies by engineering (3) _____ and industry, all engineering disciplines have been affected by technological advances. In areas like advanced electronics or IT, technical knowledge can rapidly become outdated. Even those who (4) _____ their education are vulnerable to layoffs if their particular technology or product becomes obsolete. By keeping up-to-date in their field, engineers can (5) _____ the best solutions and offer the greatest value to employers. Engineers who have not kept current in their field may be passed over for (6) _____ or be vulnerable to layoffs. However, high-tech areas often offer great challenges, interesting work, and high salaries. So engineers, when making career choices, need to (7) _____ not only the potential rewards but also the risk of technological (8) _____.

i Look for up-to-date statistics about employment prospects for graduates in your field and present your findings in a report, complete with any relevant graphs, charts, etc.

Task:
Organize a careers fair

The company you work for is interested in recruiting science and engineering graduates. You have been asked to organize a careers fair for college students in their senior year.

With your team:

1. Decide what sort of science and engineering careers to focus on.

2. Decide on the length and scope of your event and choose a suitable venue.

3. Decide what sort of presentations, talks, plenaries, workshops, panel sessions, etc., you wish to include. Also include details of any social events or fun activities that you wish to include.

4. Draw up a list of the specialists and experts that you would like to invite to participate in the event.

5. Decide if you wish to include special events aimed at recruiting women into the world of science and engineering and, if so, plan these events.

6. Discuss which aspects of science and engineering careers you wish to give most attention to: job satisfaction, salaries, current and future prospects, professional advancement, challenge, etc.

7. Present your finished proposal for the careers fair complete with any relevant diagrams, charts, lists, etc.

Review 1

A Complete the sentences with the appropriate *relative pronoun*.

1. Many people consider Michael Faraday to have been the man _____ experiments opened the door to the field of electrical engineering.
2. Infrared rays are electromagnetic waves _____ have wavelengths longer than those of red light.
3. The Caribbean is the area _____ hurricanes occur most frequently.
4. Nobody really knows the reason _____ ice ages occur.
5. I'm not sure that your proposal is _____ we need at this time.

B Combine the sentences with a *connecting phrase*.

1. Lightning causes chemical changes in the air. _____, nitrates are washed into the soil by rain.
2. Most reactions convert reactants completely into products. _____, this is not always the case.
3. Some scientists want to clone human embryos _____ get replacement tissues for people who need them.
4. _____ the earth's axis is tilted relative to its orbit, we get the changing of seasons.
5. When a gas is heated, it expands, becoming less dense, _____ it rises.

C Complete the crossword with the missing words.

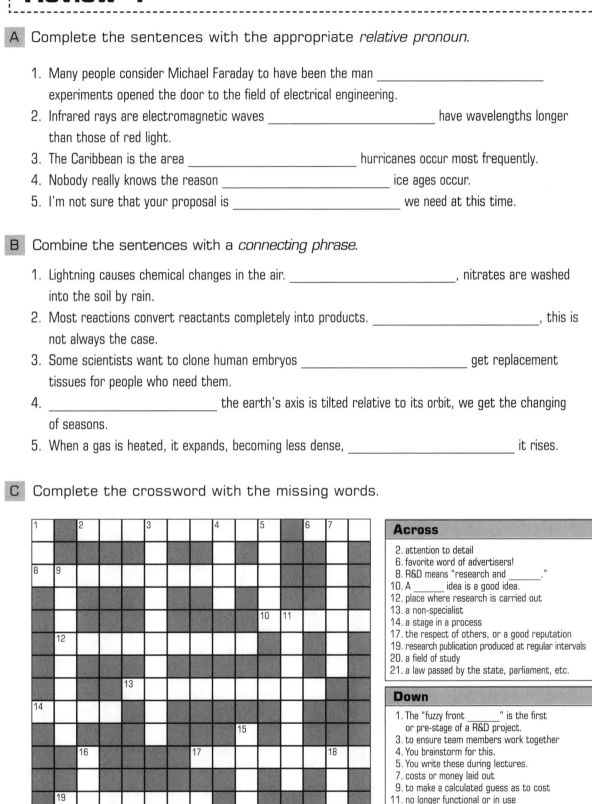

Across

2. attention to detail
6. favorite word of advertisers!
8. R&D means "research and _____."
10. A _____ idea is a good idea.
12. place where research is carried out
13. a non-specialist
14. a stage in a process
17. the respect of others, or a good reputation
19. research publication produced at regular intervals
20. a field of study
21. a law passed by the state, parliament, etc.

Down

1. The "fuzzy front _____" is the first or pre-stage of a R&D project.
3. to ensure team members work together
4. You brainstorm for this.
5. You write these during lectures.
7. costs or money laid out
9. to make a calculated guess as to cost
11. no longer functional or in use
15. tool or machine
16. A "_____-functional" approach involves people from different fields working together.
18. money given by a state for research

Review 2

A Complete the sentences with the *verb* in the appropriate tense and voice.

1. Smoking _____ (not allow) anywhere in the building.
2. Newcomen's steam engines _____ (employ) to pump water from mines.
3. By the start of the Civil War 30,000 miles of railroad track _____ (lay) in the United States.
4. Increasingly, glass fibers _____ (use) for long-distance telephone links.
5. It _____ (hope) that a cheap renewable energy source _____ (find) soon.

B Put the *verbs* into the correct form and then match the clauses.

A	B
1. If the polar ice caps _____ (melt),	a. many more lives _____ (lose) in World War II.
2. If a building _____ (insulate),	b. they _____ (can be) a major energy resource in the twenty-first century.
3. If penicillin _____ (discover) in 1929,	c. sea levels would rise and low-lying areas of the world _____ (flood).
4. If capital costs and efficiency of solar panels _____ (improve),	d. some experts think that global temperatures _____ (rise) by several degrees in the next few decades.
5. Unless carbon dioxide emissions _____ (reduce) soon,	e. less energy _____ (flow) out of it and thus heating costs will go down.

C Complete the sentences with a suitable word from the box. Use the plural form if necessary. One word is not used.

aviation	module	playtest	subassembly	trilemma	value	welding

1. One of the main aims of _____ engineering is to increase the ratio of function to cost.
2. _____ are conducted on computer games before they are put on the market.
3. _____ engineering is concerned with the design and production of aircraft.
4. Trying to satisfy three criteria - for example, high quality, low cost and speed of production - when only two can realistically be met is a classic _____.
5. _____ and _____ are examples of multipurpose components that can be adapted easily for use in a variety of manufactured products.

A Complete the sentences with the correct form of the *simple present* or *present continuous* verb.

1. Our company _____ (manufacture) household goods. At the moment I _____ (work) on a condenser for a new refrigerator.
2. The Red Sea _____ (form) part of the Great Rift Valley fault. At this point in history it _____ (widen) at a rate of approximately half an inch per year.
3. Acme Avionics _____ (specialize) in missile guidance systems for the Air Force. They currently _____ (invest) heavily in research.
4. Modern astrophysics _____ (tell) us that galaxies _____ (fly) apart, somewhat like dots on the surface of an expanding balloon.
5. Despite the fact that fossil fuels _____ (run out), they still _____ (provide) most of our energy.

B Complete the sentences with the appropriate *preposition*.

1. I'm absolutely useless _____ chess. I've never won a game in my life.
2. Naturally her parents were delighted _____ her exam results.
3. My brother is responsible _____ the quality assurance aspect of the process.
4. The color of the resulting solution depends _____ the acidity.
5. I don't think they are aware _____ the potential dangers.

C Match the branch of study with the object of study. One of the words is not a branch of study.

branch of study		object of study
1. dynamics	_____	a. systems in a state of rest
2. ergonomics	_____	b. electronics with mechanical engineering
3. kinematics	_____	c. motion and machinery
4. logistics	_____	d. force and motion
5. mechanics	_____	e. design for human comfort
6. mechatronics	_____	f. energy and environment
7. statics	_____	g. motion without considering the forces responsible
8. thermodynamics	_____	

Review 4

A Combine the two sentences to make a longer *conditional* sentence in the *past*.

1. You didn't attend the meeting. You didn't have the chance to vote.

   If _____ , you _____ .

2. She got altitude sickness. She didn't make it to the summit of Everest.

   If _____ , she _____ .

3. The heat-shielding tiles were damaged at take-off. *Columbia* burned up on re-entry.

   If _____ , _____ .

B Complete the sentences with the appropriate preposition.

1. She dropped _____ of college to join the Peace Corps.

2. He showed _____ late for the exam and was turned _____ .

3. We need to come _____ _____ some ideas pretty quickly.

4. It was my difficulty _____ physics that put me _____ studying medicine.

C Complete the sentences with an appropriate verb.

1. To save time and trouble, I try to _____ traveling during the rush hour.

2. A well-known motivating technique is to get people to _____ themselves winning.

3. If we put it under any more stress we _____ damaging the whole structure.

4. They decided to _____ making the appointment since none of the candidates were _____ suitable.

D Complete the sentences with the word from the box that describes the type of engineer.

production	electronic	maintenance	operating	quality control	safety

1. I work as a _____ engineer. Our main objective is to prevent accidents.

2. My responsibilities as a _____ engineer include timely and efficient repairs.

3. As a _____ engineer I have to check that all systems meet various technical requirements.

4. _____ engineers have to ensure that everything runs in a reliable and economic way.

5. Jim's a _____ engineer. Today he's coordinating the installation of heavy machinery at a new truck manufacturing plant.

A Complete the sentences with the *present perfect simple* or *continuous*.

1. _____ you _____ (finish) that report yet? What _____ you _____ (do)?
2. Sorry I'm late. I'_____ (talk) to the boss.
3. _____ you ever _____ (experience) a severe earthquake?

B Complete the *conditional* sentences. More than one answer is possible.

1. If you want to teach at a university, you should first _____.
2. If you heat a mixture of sulfur and rubber, cross-linking _____, which _____ the rubber to harden.
3. If you have been in the engineering profession for a while, you _____ some important trends such as licensure and an interdisciplinary approach.

C Underline the correct option in each sentence.

1. I enjoy (studying / to study) and (learning / to learn). I guess I just love (being / to be) a student.
2. With my expenses I cannot afford (taking / to take) a cut in salary.
3. It looks like they've managed (getting / to get) permission to demolish the building.
4. Dr. Higgins thinks we should consider (redesigning / to redesign) the whole structure.

D Complete the crossword. The words are all about studying and the workplace!

Across

1. "computer aided design"
5. oral examination of a job or college applicant
8. job layoff
10. field of highly educated & trained people
11. dissertation or exam
14. one holding a B.S.
16. first writing of a plan, essay or book
18. universal mental picture, usually incorrect
20. to watch or supervise
21. path through life in a chosen profession
22. permission granted by state or government to practice a profession

Down

2. dissuade or deter
3. look at again, study
4. _____ only comes with experience!
6. what companies and Olympic athletes do!
7. opposite of "layperson"
9. kick out of a job
12. intermediary body e.g., for employment
13. advancement to higher position in a company
15. the world of learning
17. personal teacher, usually one to one
19. general tendency or direction

Unit 1

Defining relative clauses

Main clause	Adjective clause
Some work is carried out by private industry	**that** employs scientists for research projects.
This is the professor	**whose** students won that research award last year.
This is the place	**where** decisions about funding are taken.
He's the kind of teacher	**who** encourages independent thinking.
A college with a strong research record is	**what** we are looking for.

- A defining relative clause identifies a person or a thing.
- *Who, that, what, where,* and *whose* are relative pronouns.
- The relative pronoun *who* is used for people and *which* is used for things.
- The relative pronoun *that* is often used instead of *who* or *which.*
- The relative pronoun *where* is used to describe places.
- The possessive pronoun *whose* is usually used to refer to people. It is always followed by a noun.
- The relative pronoun *what* means "the thing(s) that." It often, though not always, goes at the beginning of a sentence.

PRACTICE

Combine the two sentences using *relative pronouns*.

1. The research institute has just obtained some new funding. I work there.

   _____

2. This is Professor Wilkinson. Professor Wilkinson's book was published last month.

   _____

3. The American Cancer Society is a well-known foundation. It is involved in disease research.

   _____

4. You need to talk with Professor Dawes. Professor Dawes handles the admissions.

   _____

5. The department has no more money for research. That is the difficult thing.

   _____

6. The application procedure is very complex. We have to follow the application procedure.

   _____

Connecting phrases

Examples

Though some R&D scientists may work alone, most work in project teams.

We use a cross-functional system **because** it works better.

His proposal was **neither** original **nor** practical.

In order to get your ideas across, you need to communicate effectively.

Their way of working was **not only** old-fashioned **but also** very inefficient.

Michael has resigned. **As a result**, we're without a project leader at the moment.

Explanations

Though is used for marking a contrast between two actions, facts, events, etc.

Because is used to say why a person does something or why something happens.

Neither and *nor* are used to show that a negative statement is true about two things.

In order to is used to express a person's purpose or intention.

Not only . . . but also is used to emphasize that a second point is also true.

As a result is used to describe the consequence(s) of an action or event.

PRACTICE
Complete the sentences with the correct *connecting phrases*.

1. The government has cut our budget. _____, we are going to have to change our plans.

2. We need to work faster _____ have the results ready by April.

3. He's _____ a very knowledgeable engineer _____ a very shrewd businessman.

4. Most of the people on the team are engineers _____ some have other backgrounds.

5. They are determined to go ahead and _____ you _____ anyone else can stop them.

6. I think Janet is the best choice for team leader _____ she has the most experience.

ABOUT YOU
Use the *connecting phrases* in the box to write three sentences about your study or work.

1. _____

2. _____

3. _____

Unit 2

Past perfect tense

Past perfect	Subject + *had* + past participle
Affirmative statement	By 1929, **he had started** his own industrial design company. Subject + *had* + past participle
Negative statement	**They had not expected** to have so much success so soon. Subject + *had* + not + past participle
Yes/no questions	**Had she worked** in industrial design before? *Had* + subject + past participle
Wh- questions	**Who had he worked for** before he joined that company? *Wh-* word + *had* + subject + past participle

- The past perfect is used to describe an action that was completed before another action or time in the past or to explain why this event happened.
- Usually, the past perfect is used for the earlier action and the simple past for the later action.
- In sentences with *before* or *after* in which a time relationship is already established, both actions can be described using the simple past tense.
  Before *I handed in the report, I checked it one last time.*
  After *the meeting, everyone felt much better about the design.*

PRACTICE
Complete the sentences with the correct tense (**simple past** or **past perfect**) of the given verbs.

1. By the time we _____ (finish) the job, we _____ (spend) over a million dollars.
2. We _____ (do) a lot of research before we _____ (start) the project.
3. I _____ (be) nervous on my first day, because I _____ (not work) for a large company before.
4. I _____ (return) from vacation and found that the plans _____ (change).

ABOUT YOU
Complete and write sentences that are true for you. Use the **past perfect** tense.

1. By the time I was twelve, I had _____
2. By the time I started high school, I had _____
3. _____
4. _____

Real conditionals in the future

Affirmative and negative statements

Condition *If* + subject + present tense verb,	Result subject + *will* + verb
If you increase the weight, If we don't fix this problem,	the cost will increase. we won't make the deadline.

Yes/no questions

If + subject + present tense verb, *will* + subject + verb	Short answer
If we reduce the cost of the materials, will this affect the quality? If we make a higher-quality product, will it be ready in time?	Yes, it will. No, it won't.

Wh- questions

If + subject + present tense verb, *wh-* word + *will* + subject + verb	Answer
If we forget about this design and start again, what will they say? If we reduce the thickness of the case, how will this affect the cost?	They'll say you're crazy! It'll go down.

- Factual conditionals describe future situations that are real or possible under certain circumstances. The *if* clause describes a condition, while the main clause describes a certain or probable result.
- The *if* clause can come first or second in the sentence:
  I'll talk to the design team if I have time later today.
  If I have time later today, I'll talk to the design team.
- When the *if* clause comes first in a sentence, it is followed by a comma.

PRACTICE

Use the cues to write sentences using **real conditionals**.

1. the company / offer / you / a job / what / you / do?

_____

2. they / approve / the budget / we / start work / next month

_____

3. we / ask for / more time / management / agree?

_____

4. we / make / product / more light-weight / it / not be / as strong

_____

Passive voice: present

Passive voice	Subject + *be* + past participle
Affirmative statement	**This score is compared** against the initial cost. Subject + *be* + past participle
Negative statement	**This material is not affected** by changes in temperature. Subject + *be* + *not* + past participle
Yes/no questions	**Are comparative tests always designed** the same way? *Be* + subject + past participle
Wh- questions	**How are LEDs used** in domestic appliances? *Wh-* word + *be* + subject + past participle

- The passive voice is used to give more emphasis to an action rather than to the person or thing that performs the action, when this person or thing is not so important, or when it is implicitly understood or is not known.
- Passive sentences usually sound more formal than active ones.
- The passive voice is very common in English and is commonly used in news reports, official documents, signs, descriptions of scientific or technical processes, etc.

PRACTICE
Rewrite each sentence using the *passive voice*.

1. They interview the candidates on three separate occasions.

_____

2. The phosphors in the diode absorb the radiation.

_____

3. Do they use LEDs in the alphanumeric displays on things like clocks?

_____

4. The phosphors in the diode absorb the radiation.

_____

5. At what stage do they carry out a comparative test?

_____

6. We assemble all the components right here in this factory.

_____

Unit 3

Simple present vs. present continuous tense

	Simple present tense	Present continuous tense
Affirmative statement	I work for an oil company.	He's preparing the experiment right now.
Negative statement	I don't write software programs.	The equipment is not functioning properly.
Yes/no questions	Do you enjoy your work?	Are you making good progress?
Wh- questions	Who do you report to?	What are you looking for?

- The simple present is used to describe regular or habitual activities and situations, to talk about facts and truths about the world, and to express relatively unchanging attitudes, feelings, and opinions.
- The present continuous is used to describe an action that is in progress at the moment of speaking.
- The present continuous can also be used to talk about a present activity or situation that may not actually be in progress at the moment of speaking.
- The following verbs, which describe states rather than actions, are not usually used in continuous forms: *believe, contain, exist, forget, hate, hear, know, like, need, prefer, realize, remember, seem, suppose, understand, want.*

PRACTICE
Complete the conversations with the correct form (**simple present** or **present continuous**) of the given verbs.

1. We _____ (manufacture) LEDs. I _____ (spend) most of the day in a clean room.
2. This company _____ (make) computer hardware. Right now, I _____ (work) on a design for a new mouse.
3. I _____ (design) navigation systems for the Air Force. At the moment, I _____ (work) on a new radar system.
4. I _____ (work) at a chemical plant. I _____ (supervise) the filtration processes.

ABOUT YOU
Write four sentences that are true for you; two in the **simple present** and two in the **present continuous**.

1. _____
2. _____
3. _____
4. _____

Simple present tense

Simple present: uses	Examples
To describe habitual activities	They finish work at six o'clock.
To state facts and general truths about the world	Scientists conduct research.
To express relatively unchanging feelings, desires, wishes, opinions	I want to start my own company one day.
To tell jokes and anecdotes	There are two engineers in a laboratory. The first one says . . .
To report news	Biochemists make important breakthrough.
To summarize the contents of a book, a report, etc.	In her article, Professor Wallis examines the role of . . .
To talk about scheduled future events	Her interview is the day after tomorrow.

- In the affirmative form, the simple present consists of a subject followed by the base form (the infinitive form) of a verb except in the case of the third person singular.
- The spelling of the third person form changes in certain cases:
  With verbs that end in *-e*, just add *-s*.
  With verbs that end in *-o*, *-sh*, *-ch*, *-ss*, *-zz*, or *-x*, add *-es*.
  With verbs that end in a consonant and *-y*, change the y to **i** and add *-es*.

PRACTICE

Complete the conversations with the correct **auxiliaries** and forms of the following verbs: *mix, teach, like, study, fix*.

1. A: What _____ your brother do?
2. B: He _____ air conditioning systems.

3. A: _____ Ann study at home?
4. B: No. She usually _____ at the library.

5. A: What _____ she do with the solvents?
6. B: She _____ them together.

7. A: Does he _____ his new job?
8. B: Yes, he does. He _____ it a lot.

9. A: Where does Professor Smith _____?
10. B: She _____ at MIT.

Adjective-preposition combinations

Adjective +	Examples
about	excited about, happy about, worried about, sorry about
at	good at, brilliant at, hopeless at, surprised at
for	responsible for, famous for, difficult for, impossible for
in	proficient in, well-versed in, expert in, interested in, involved in
of	aware of, capable of, full of, short of
with	conversant with, acquainted with, familiar with, pleased with, disappointed with

- Certain adjectives can be combined with more than one preposition and each combination has a separate meaning.

    I'm **sorry about** the decision but there's nothing we can do.

    I feel **sorry for** the members of the team. A lot of their work was wasted.

PRACTICE
Complete each space with an appropriate **adjective**.

1. Thomas Edison is _____ for the great number of inventions he patented.
2. She had been absent and so she wasn't _____ of the seriousness of the situation.
3. We were _____ with the results. They weren't as good as we had expected.
4. My brother is absolutely _____ at solving complex problems. He's a genius!
5. We're all very _____ about the new project. It's going to very interesting.
6. She is _____ for supervising the quality control in the whole production process.
7. I think they are perfectly _____ of making up their own minds.
8. The team worked very well together. I was very _____ with their performance.

ABOUT YOU
Complete and write sentences that are true for you. Use the expressions in the chart.

1. I am interested in _____
2. I'm not very familiar with _____
3. _____
4. _____
5. _____

Unit 4

Unreal conditionals in the past

Condition *If* + subject + *had* + past participle	Result subject + *would have* + past participle
If the weather had been warmer that day,	the O-ring would not have become brittle.
If Fleming hadn't noticed the bacteria,	he wouldn't have discovered penicillin.

Yes/no questions

If + subject + *had* + past participle, *would* + subject + *have* + past participle
If you had applied to graduate school, would they have accepted you? If they had started the project earlier, would they have finished by now?

Wh- questions

If + subject + *had* + past participle, *wh-* word + *would* + subject + *have* + past participle
If the experiment had gone wrong, who would you have called for help? If they hadn't provided funding for the project, what would we have done?

- Unreal conditionals in the past are used to describe events that did not happen or situations that did not exist in the past. The *if* clause describes a hypothetical, i.e., unreal condition, while the main clause describes a hypothetical result.
- The *if* clause can come first or second in the sentence:
    If you had known about the grant, would you have applied for it?
    Would you have applied for the grant if *you had known about it*?
- When the *if* clause comes first in a sentence, it is followed by a comma.

PRACTICE
Complete the sentences with the correct form of the given verbs.

1. We _____ (win) that award if we _____ (work) a bit harder.
2. If we _____ (not take) the same science course, we _____ (never meet).
3. I _____ (prepare) some material if I _____ (know) you were coming.
4. He _____ (not hear) about the change of plan if she _____ (not tell) him.
5. If the SRB _____ (not break) off, the fuel tank _____ (not explode).
6. If I _____ (knew) he was going to object, I _____ (be) more tactful.
7. If he _____ (stay) on that course, he _____ (be) very unhappy.
8. You _____ (receive) the report if you _____ (arrive) earlier.

Phrasal verbs

- Phrasal verbs consist of a verb plus a preposition and/or an adverb. Some phrasal verbs are intransitive, that is, they have no object.

    The machine has **broken down** again.

    Please **speak up**. I can't hear you.

    The price of oil is **going up**.

- Some two-part phrasal verbs can be separated. The object can go in either of two positions.

    She **pointed out** the problem to me.

    She **pointed** the problem **out** to me.

- But if a pronoun is used, it must separate the two parts of the phrasal verb.

    She **pointed** it **out** to me.

- Some two-part phrasal verbs cannot be separated.

    He **took to** engineering immediately.

- Multi-word verbs consist of a verb, an adverb and a preposition. They can never be separated and they always take a direct object.

    We need to **come up with** a new design.

    I think we should **get rid of** that old machinery.

PRACTICE 1
Underline the one incorrect sentence in each group.

1. They turned the generator on.	They turned it on.	They turned on it.
2. We are looking the answer for.	We are looking for it.	We are looking for the answer.
3. She gave the money back.	She gave back the money.	She gave back it.
4. He turned down the offer.	He turned down it.	He turned the offer down.
5. I picked up them.	I picked up the reports.	I picked the reports up.
6. Get on with your work.	Get with your work on.	Get on with it.

PRACTICE 2
Complete the sentences with the correct verbs.

1. Many girls _____ out of math and science courses during middle school or high school.
2. They _____ for ways to improve the safety and efficiency of the equipment.
3. Negative messages about science tend to _____ girls off.
4. We are trying to _____ down the risk of accidents in the workplace.
5. He _____ away a golden opportunity when he turned down that job.

Modals for prohibition, obligation, and permission

Modal	Example	Meaning
must	Drivers **must** wear seatbelts.	This is necessary and obligatory.
have to	They **have to** work in a clean room.	This is necessary and obligatory.
mustn't	You **mustn't** smoke in here.	This is prohibited.
not have to	I **don't have to** wear a suit at the office.	This is not obligatory. It is optional.
can	You **can** eat in the canteen if you want to.	This is permitted. It is not obligatory.

- *Must*, *mustn't*, and *can* are followed by the infinitive form of a verb without to.
- The forms of *must*, *mustn't*, and *can* do not change, whoever the subject is.
- The forms of *have to* and *not have to* change for the third person singular.
- *Must* and *have to* are often interchangeable. But when asking questions about things that are necessary or obligatory, have to is much more commonly used.
- *Mustn't* and *not have to* do not mean the same and are not interchangeable.

PRACTICE
Complete each space with an appropriate expression.

1. We _____ wear special clothing to protect us from harmful radiation.
2. You _____ let any dust come into contact with the components.
3. Of course, you _____ wear a tie if you want to but it's not compulsory.
4. Did you _____ wear a school uniform when you were younger?
5. Safety is very important in this factory. You _____ wear a hard hat at all times.
6. We _____ use the mask and the gloves when we are outside the clean room.

ABOUT YOU
For each expression, write a sentence that is true about your school or place of work.

1. can _____
2. have to _____
3. must _____
4. mustn't _____
5. not have to _____

Verb combinations with gerund forms

Verbs that form combinations with gerunds		Examples
avoid	go on	
be no good	be used to	Have you considered moving to another company?
consider	be worth	He's used to working under pressure.
delay	keep on	I don't want to risk missing the deadline.
dislike	postpone	I can envisage restructuring the whole operation.
enjoy	resume	Have you finished checking those figures yet?
envisage	risk	
finish	suggest	
give up	think about	

PRACTICE
Complete each sentence with the correct form of one of the expressions from the box.

1. If we don't update and improve our products, we _____ losing sales.
2. They soon fixed the problem and were able to _____ working quite quickly.
3. Plan A is good, I admit. But Plan B is also _____ thinking about.
4. We implemented a quality control program, but sales _____ on falling.
5. My boss, like most bosses, _____ being interrupted.
6. This component is not working. Maybe we should _____ redesigning it.
7. I think we should _____ taking a final decision until we have seen more data.

ABOUT YOU
Complete and write sentences that are true for you. Use expressions from the box.

1. In my experience, it's not worth _____
2. In my spare time, I enjoy _____
3. In this country, people are used to _____
4. _____
5. _____
6. _____

Unit 5

Present perfect tense

Present perfect	subject + *has/have* + past participle
Affirmative statement	**I have seen** many changes over the last few years. subject + *has/have* + past participle
Negative statement	**They have not worked** outside this country before. subject + *has/have* + *not* + past participle
Yes/no questions	**Has he taken** his professional exams? *has/have* + subject + past participle
Wh- questions	**How has CAD software changed** the way you work? *Wh-* word + *has/have* + subject + past participle

Use the present perfect tense:
- to show that something happened at an unspecified time in the past
- to show that something happened more than once in the past
- to show that something started at a specific time in the past and continues now

PRACTICE

Use the cues to complete the sentences and questions in the **present perfect** tense.

1. you / write   _____ any application letters?
2. I / draw   _____ a sketch of how I think the design should be.
3. stresses / break   _____ the seals on the fuel tanks.
4. you / hear   _____ about the latest CAD software?
5. the government / cut   _____ funding for research in this area.
6. he / be   _____ a civil engineer for twenty-two years.

ABOUT YOU

Use the **present perfect** to write true sentences about things that you have and have not done.

1. _____
2. _____
3. _____
4. _____

Will for predictions

Will	subject + *will* + base form
Affirmative statement	**Computers will become** more and more powerful. subject + *will* + base form
Negative statement	**Videoconferencing won't replace** face-to-face meetings. subject + *will* + *not* + base form
Yes/no questions	**Will you stay** in the same field? *will* + subject + base form
Wh- questions	**How will engineering courses be** in the future? *Wh-* word + *will* + subject + base form

- ▪ *Will* is used for simple predictions about future actions or situations.
- ▪ *Will* is often used with expressions like *probably, (I'm) sure, (I) think, (I) doubt, (I) guess,* etc.

PRACTICE
Use the cues to write predictions using *will*.

1. computers / solar-powered _____
2. some of my friends / work / abroad _____
3. principal source of energy / wind _____
4. specialization / increase _____

ABOUT YOU
Using *will*, write your own predictions about the following topics.

1. the role of computers in your chosen field

_____

2. the number and status of women working in your chosen field

_____

3. science and engineering education

_____

4. employment prospects for science and engineering graduates

_____

Real conditionals in the present

If + subject + present tense verb,	subject + present tense verb
If air expands, If you're an engineer, If you have completed a science degree,	it becomes lighter. you know all about forces, mechanics, hydraulics, etc. you have proved that you can think analytically.

If + subject + present tense verb,	subject + modal verb
If you are a chemist, If your field is biology, If you have other interests outside science,	you could work for a pharmaceutical company. you might find yourself working in the biomedical field. you may find it easier to make a career change.

If + subject + present tense verb,	imperative
But if you want to do well, If you're interested in energy,	learn how to work in a team. think about a career in electrical engineering.

- Present factual conditionals are used to talk about general truths and scientific facts.
- Present factual conditional can also be used to describe things that happen again and again.
- Present factual conditionals with modals can be used to express ability, possibility, advisability, etc.
- Present factual conditionals can be combined with imperatives to give instructions and commands.
- The *if* clause can come first or second in the sentence:
    If it is exposed to the air, it becomes oxidized.
    It becomes oxidized *if it is exposed to the air.*
When the *if* clause comes first in a sentence, it is followed by a comma.

PRACTICE
Complete each *real conditional* sentence in an appropriate way.

1. Those courses are all the same. If you've taken one, _____
2. If you're in your final year of college, you probably _____
3. If you want to get a good engineering job, _____
4. If you are working in the private sector, _____
5. If you've decided to do a PhD, you've probably _____
6. If you mix salt and water, _____
7. If you have a physics degree, you could _____

Verb combinations with infinitive forms

Verbs that form combinations with infinitives		Examples
afford	expect	
agree	help	He claims to be the best person for the job.
aim	hope	Finally, they consented to talk about the proposal.
appear	manage	The question is whether we can afford to do it.
arrange	need	It appears to be some sort of semiconductor.
choose	omit	This company aims to manufacture the best
claim	promise	products on the market.
consent	refuse	
decide	tend	
demand	threaten	

PRACTICE

Underline the correct option, in each sentence.

1. I enjoy (seeing / to see) a project through to completion.
2. Sometimes I ask myself, "Is it worth (to stay / staying) here?"
3. In the end, we managed (to improve / improving) the efficiency of the engine.
4. The company is considering (moving / to move) the factory to another site.
5. We expect (seeing / to see) a big improvement in quality.
6. She was so angry that she threatened (to resign / resigning).
7. It's no good (complaining / to complain) now that the decision has been made.
8. I've arranged (having / to have) the prototype tested externally.

ABOUT YOU

Complete the sentences so that they are true for you.

1. I have recently decided to _____
2. I'm flexible, but one thing I refuse to do is _____
3. Five years from now, I hope to _____
4. I confess that one thing I tend to do is _____

Glossary

Note: The definitions given in the glossary are specific to the context in which they are used in **English for Science and Engineering**.
For a more general definition, the reader is advised to consult a dictionary.

		Unit	Meaning	Example
absorb	*v t*	3	**1** to soak up, take in **2** to accept a loss (expense, punishment)	*1 The sponge absorbed water from the sink.* *2 Sending the wrong refrigerator was our mistake, so we'll absorb the cost of sending the right one.*
adsorb	*v t*	3	to hold on or stick to the surface of a solid or liquid	*Raindrops are adsorbed onto the surface of window panes.*
algorithm	*n*	3	a series of steps or instructions to do something specific	*Systems analysts use algorithms that computer programmers can follow.*
appliance	*n*	2	a device used for a specific function, usually electrical and in the home	*Major appliances include stoves, refrigerators, washing machines, and dishwashers.*
assembly	*n*	2	putting parts of something together	*The assembly of a rifle by a soldier can be done in seconds.*
attribute listing	*n*	1	an idea-generating technique whereby a product is broken down into its components and the properties of each one are then examined with a view to its improvement (c.f. **virtual prototyping**)	*Attribute listing is generally used in conjunction with other creative techniques like brainstorming.*
aviation engineering	*n*	2	design and manufacture of aircraft, especially airplanes	*The field of aviation engineering is well paid.*
beta version	*n*	2	version of a new product in the final stages just before marketing	*Beta testing of a computer game is done with a limited form of the game just to pick up any last-minute problems.*
blueprint	*n*	5	a detailed drawing of something to show how to make it; a plan; a pattern	*Workers read blueprints to see how to construct a building.*
booster	*n*	4	the part of a rocket that contains fuel and an engine to send it into space	*The booster rocket for the Apollo missions was the Saturn V.*
brainstorm	*v t*	1	to think of as many ideas as possible without criticizing them	*Every month, we brainstorm ideas for new products.*
bug	*n*	2	a fault in an electrical or mechanical device or system	*My computer program has a bug in it; every time I type "n," it goes to the bottom of the page.*
CAD	*n*	2	Computer Aided Design	
commission	*n*	4	a group of people authorized, usually by a government, to do something	*The town council created a commission to protect its historical landmarks.*
configure	*v t*	3	to design or make ready a device or machine for a particular use	*The tank is configured for certain battle operations.*
consumer goods	*n* *pl*	2	articles necessary for daily living, such as food, clothes, and everyday things	*The market for consumer goods is huge, but so is the competition.*
critical path (method)	*n*	1	a method in R&D whereby a project is broken down into steps and sequences to determine the minimum time required	*The Critical Path Method (CPM) was developed by the DuPont Corporation in the 1950s.*
crystallization	*n*	3	the process of forming a liquid into crystals	*Crystallization of cloud moisture into snow occurs at high altitudes.*
data	*n* *pl*	1	raw or organized information; numbers; facts	*Scientists gather data, then study it for its meaning. Computers process data to create information.*

		Unit	Meaning	Example
device	*n*	1	**1** an electrical or mechanical machine **2** a tool or implement	*Major appliances include stoves, refrigerators, washing machines, and dishwashers.*
diode	*n*	3	**1** an electronic device that causes current to flow in one direction **2** an electron tube with a cathode and an anode **3** a two-terminal semiconductor device used mainly as a rectifier	*A diode is essentially an electronic valve.*
discipline	*n*	1	a field of study	*In which discipline does that teacher work? She teaches mathematics.*
dissolution	*n*	3	**1** the act of dissolving; putting solid into a liquid and making it seem to disappear **2** breaking up a larger piece into tiny fragments	*The higher the temperature, the faster the dissolution of sugar in water.*
distillation	*n*	3	method of separating the components of a solution according to their different boiling points	*Distillation is an important process in the manufacture of perfumes.*
durable	*adj.*	2	hard-wearing; long-lasting; sturdy	*The soles on those shoes have lasted a year; they are quite durable.*
dynamics	*n*	3	the study of force and motion (c.f. **kinematics**)	*The main practical applications of dynamics are found in aerodynamics and hydrodynamics.*
economics	*n*	1	the study of how society uses resources, such as money, labor, raw materials, and factories	*Economics is at the center of most governmental concerns.*
electrical engineering	*n*	2	the design and production of electrical systems and equipment	*Electrical engineering became a recognized field in the late nineteenth century with the need for large-scale generation of electricity.*
engineering	*n*	1	**1** the profession of an engineer **2** the scientific planning of a machine, road, bridge, etc.	*Students who like problem-solving are good candidates for a career in engineering.*
ergonomics	*n*	3	the study of the best way to design machines for human comfort, convenience, and business efficiency	*She is an expert in computer ergonomics.*
evaporate	*v i*	3	to change from a liquid into a vapor	*Water evaporates from lakes and oceans.*
facility	*n*	3	the site and equipment for manufacturing; a factory (see **plant**)	*An industrial engineer may be responsible for the design and implementation of an industrial facility.*
filtration	*n*	3	a method of separating mixtures according to the different particle sizes	*Filtration is one of the first steps in the process of water purification.*
foundation	*n*	1	an organization, usually nonprofit, that provides money for projects in education, politics, science, and the arts	*The Ford Foundation supports many educational projects.*
fuzzy front end	*n*	1	the first phase in the product-development cycle when ideas are generated	*Some people consider the "fuzzy front end" to be part of the R&D process while others regard it as something that happens prior to development.*
generator	*n*	3	a machine used to produce electricity	*The hospital has two emergency generators in case of a power cut.*
hands-on	*adj.*	1	practical rather than theoretical; involving direct experience	*The course offers hands-on experience in the use of computers.*

		Unit	Meaning	Example
hard hat	*n*	**4**	a protective helmet usually worn by civil engineers	*The company insists that everyone visiting the construction site wear a hard hat.*
hardware	*n*	**2**	the visible parts of a computer or computer system (c.f. **software**)	*The hardware includes the monitor, tower, mouse, keyboard and printer, and all their components.*
high-tech	*adj.*	**1**	using complex engineering, usually in the latest technology	*Advances in computer technology need high-tech solutions.*
human-factors engineering	*n*	**5**	human-centered design of parts and machines that stresses comfort, efficiency, and safety (see also **ergonomics** and **time-study engineering**)	*The field of human-factors engineering has expanded in recent years.*
humidify	*v t*	**3**	to make the atmosphere in an enclosed space more humid or moist	*Scientists have found that humidifying the air in the home, factory, or office helps people who suffer from asthma.*
induction	*n*	**2**	the creation of a voltage or current by moving a conductor in a magnetic field	*The power needs of the country depend on electromagnetic induction to generate electricity and on the power distribution grid to supply it to homes and workplaces.*
industrial design	*n*	**2**	the design of mass-produced items to improve aesthetic appeal and usability	*A number of countries have signed up with the Hague Agreement, which offers protection of rights to industrial designers.*
innovation	*n*	**1**	something new, made or improved with creativity	*Cellular telephones were an innovation in the 1990s, but now they are very common.*
install	*v t*	**3**	to put something (such as a piece of machinery) in place and make it work	*Our technical expert installed a new computer Wednesday, and we began using it Friday.*
integrated circuit	*n*	**3**	a miniaturized electronic circuit made out of semiconductor material; also known as IC, microchip, silicon chip, or chip	*Integrated circuits are used in an enormous number of devices, including audio and video equipment, household utilities, and automobiles.*
invention	*n*	**1**	something useful created by someone	*After the invention of the wheel, people could travel faster.*
inventory	*n*	**2**	the total assets of a company	*The new equipment will need to be added to the inventory.*
journal	*n*	**1**	a collection of research reports in a specialized field of study	*The* New England Journal of Medicine *is for doctors and nurses.*
kinematics	*n*	**3**	the branch of mechanics that deals with the motion without considering the forces behind the motion (c.f. **dynamics**)	*Speed, velocity, and acceleration are important concepts in kinematics.*
laboratory	*n*	**1**	a specially equipped room for doing experiments and other exploratory work	*Scientists develop new products in the laboratory.*
layperson	*n*	**1**	someone who is not a specialist	*Could you please explain how the machine works so that it could be understood by the average layperson?*
LED (light-emitting diode)	*n*	**3**	a semiconductor diode that converts electricity into light for digital display	*LEDs are essential components of many electronic goods such as watches, cameras and calculators.*
licensure	*n*	**5**	the granting of a license, usually by a state, that enables the holder to practice a profession	*Most states recognize licensure from other states.*

		Unit	Meaning	Example
limit state	*n*	4	a set of performance criteria that must be met when a structure like a building or bridge is subject to loads	*Limit state criteria cover attributes such as strength, tendency to vibrate, stability, tendency to buckle or twist, and so on.*
logistics	*n*	3	the organization and distribution of goods, services, and personnel, especially in large amounts	*The logistics of moving an army into combat are very complex.*
manufacturing	*n*	1	the part of industry that makes things	*Manufacturing has left the big cities and relocated overseas.*
marketing	*n*	1	the art and science of designing, advertising, and selling goods and services	*She has a master's degree in marketing from Stanford University.*
mechanical engineering	*n*	2	the design, construction and repair of machines and systems	*Mechanical engineers can take credit for the success of many factories.*
mechanics	*n*	3	**1** the science of motion **2** the science of machinery	*The problems of mechanics are usually addressed in the laboratory.*
mechatronics	*n*	3	technology that combines electronics and mechanical engineering to develop new manufacturing methods	*Many efficient manufacturing methods depend on mechatronics for their success.*
module	*n*	2	**1** a part of a whole, such as a section in a course **2** a section of a space vehicle	*1 Our English course is divided into modules on poetry, drama, and novels. 2 The passenger module released from the rocket after takeoff.*
monitor	*n*	3	**1** a screen, as on a television or computer, that displays information **2** a person or machine that checks on the performance of something	*A computer monitor is both an input and an output device.*
NASA	*n*	4	National Aeronautics and Space Administration	
navigation	*n*	1	the science or practice of figuring out a correct course (path, route) for a ship or airplane	*Navigation of a ship across the ocean requires skill.*
obsolescence	*n*	2	the process of becoming no longer useful	*Obsolescence of buildings happens over many years, as they become too old to use.*
O-ring	*n*	4	a gasket in the form of a ring with a circular cross-section	*O-rings are one of the most common seals used in machines since they are cheap, reliable, and can withstand very high pressures.*
patent	*n*	1	the exclusive right given by a government to make, use, and sell an invention for a limited number of years	*He wanted a patent for his invention so no one else could copy it.*
PDCA	*n*	4	Plan Do Check Act	
periodical	*n*	1	a magazine or other publication that comes out at regular intervals (e.g., weekly, monthly)	*She subscribes to several periodicals.*
pharmaceutical	*n*	1	a drug or medicine	*Pharmaceuticals are sold through drugstores.*
phase	*n*	1	a period of time within a longer process of change; a stage of development	*The time you spend in high school is an important phase of your education.*
phosphor	*n*	3	a chemical that exhibits phosphorescence, i.e., sustained light emission without external stimulus	*Phosphors are transition metal compounds or rare-earth metal compounds.*
plant	*n*	3	a factory; buildings and equipment for carrying out manufacturing	*The company opened a new industrial plant for the manufacture of heavy machinery.*
plateau	*n*	1	a stage or period in which there is no change or progress	*The economy kept improving and then reached a plateau.*

		Unit	Meaning	Example
playtest	*n*	2	testing a new computer game for bugs and improvements by playing it	*Playtests are an established part of the quality control process for computer games.*
plenary	*n*	5	**1** a meeting of all fully qualified members of an organization **2** a major speech at a professional conference	*1 The United Nations is in a plenary session today. 2 Professor Plum is giving a plenary address on some new research in physics today at 2:00.*
polymerization	*n*	3	the chemical process whereby identical small molecules (called **monomers**) are joined to form long-chain molecules called polymers	*Plastics, e.g., nylon and polyethylene, are synthetic polymers.*
precision	*n*	1	attention to detail	*1 Parts of machines are made to precision. 2 The professor spoke with precision.*
propellant	*n*	4	any material that provides force for motion	*Chemical propellants usually consist of high-energy chemicals plus an oxidizing agent.*
proposal	*n*	1	**1** an offer **2** something that is suggested as a possible plan	*A competitor made a proposal to buy my business.*
prototype	*n*	2	a working model of a machine or other object used to test it before producing the final version	*Construction of the two Concorde prototypes, 001 and 002, began in the 1960s.*
publication	*n*	1	**1** a book, magazine, newspaper, etc. **2** an act of publishing something	*1 She reads all the publications in the field of medicine. 2 Publication of the novel will take place next month.*
quality assurance (quality control)	*n*	4	the testing by a company of its own products for possible problems	*Businesses use quality assurance to make sure that their products look good and work well.*
R&D (R.&D.)	*n*	1	research and development	*Some companies send huge sums of money on R&D.*
radar	*n*	3	a system or device that bounces radio waves off an object to get information about the object's location, speed, size, etc.	*Major airports use radar to control air traffic.*
raw materials	*n*	3	materials from which manufactured products are made	*Iron ore is one of the raw materials used to make steel.*
rectifier	*n*	3	an electrical device that allows current to flow more in one direction by changing AC to DC (see also **diode**)	
resistor	*n*	2	a device used to reduce the flow of an electric current	*Resistors have many applications, including heaters, fuses and audio volume controls.*
review	*n*	1	**1** a repetition of or a look back at something **2** an analysis, critique or reconsideration **3** a journal or specialist publication	*1 Our teacher did a review of last week's lesson before we took the test. 2 The plans for the new factory are under review.*
robot	*n*	3	any of a variety of devices, some with humanlike characteristics, programmed to perform various chores	*Carmakers use robots to do unpleasant jobs, such as painting cars in hot conditions.*
semiconductor	*n*	3	a material with electrical conductivity that is intermediate between that of an insulator and a conductor	*Silicon is a very commonly used semiconductor; hence the "silicon chip."*
silicon chip	*n*	3	(see **integrated circuit**)	
simulation	*n*	5	an imitation of a real situation	*The pilots learned to fly airplanes by watching ground simulations.*

	Unit		Meaning	Example
software	*n*	**2**	in a computer, a set of instructions that allows a user to perform certain tasks, such as word processing or reading information on the Internet; software is not part of the machine itself (c.f. **hardware**)	*I use communications software to exchange knowledge with other computer users.*
SPC	*n*	**4**	Statistical Process Control	
specifications	*n* *pl*	**4**	the exact details (of a product or service), usually in writing or drawn plans	*Automobiles are built to exact specifications.*
SRB	*n*	**4**	Solid-Propellant Rocket Booster	
statics	*n*	**3**	the branch of physics concerned with systems in a state where the components and structures are at rest	*Statics has common applications in the fields of structural engineering and hydrostatics.*
subassembly	*n*	**2**	an assembled unit designed to fit with other units to make a finished product	*Using multipurpose subassemblies can result in big savings on original engineering and design costs.*
telecommunications	*n*	**1**	transmission of messages and images by radio, television, cable, satellite, computer, etc.	*Telecommunications is a complex and growing field.*
thermodynamics	*n*	**3**	the branch of physics that deals with the relationship between energy and movement	*There are four laws of thermodynamics.*
timescale (time scale)	*n*	**1**	the length of time estimated for a series of events in a process or viewed as part of a longer period of time	*When put onto the geological timescale, human history is just a brief moment and the twentieth century a mere blip.*
time-study engineering	*n*	**5**	an approach to engineering design that stresses efficiency and speed (c.f. **human-factors engineering** & **ergonomics**)	*Time-study engineering is related to human-factors engineering in that both try to improve efficiency through more human-centered design.*
torsion	*n*	**4**	the stress or deformation caused when an object is twisted about its axis	*Torsion forces are practically zero in trussed beam bridges and arched bridges.*
trilemma	*n*	**2**	a three-part problem where any two criteria can be met, but not all three	*The trilemma in this case is that we need a high-quality, low-cost product in a short time.*
turbine	*n*	**3**	a machine that produces power by turning blades with steam, water, or gas, especially to create electricity	*Huge steam turbines can produce electricity for an entire city.*
utility	*n*	**3**	**1** any basic necessity or service, such as running water, electricity, or gas **2** a business or facility that supplies water, electricity, etc.	*1. Our utilities are shut off for repair, so we can't shower. 2. The local electric company is a utility.*
vacuum tube	*n*	**3**	a device used to amplify or modify a signal by controlling the movement of electrons in an evacuated space (outside U.S.: **thermionic valve**)	*Vacuum tubes were supplanted by transistors in radio and TV sets.*
value engineering (VE)	*n*	**2**	an analysis of the functions of a product, program or service aimed at improving quality and reducing costs	*VE was developed by General Electric during WW2 and is now widely used in government and industry.*
virtual prototyping	*n*	**1**	a development technique whereby a computer-based simulation is used in place of a physical prototype for test and evaluation of a new design (c.f. **attribute listing**)	*In the field of aircraft design, virtual prototyping is used nowadays instead of the more costly and time-consuming wind tunnel testing.*
weld	*v t*	**2**	to join metal things by melting them slightly and putting them together	*Welding steel plates together is an important part of the shipbuilding process.*

Audio Script

CD
T-1

Unit 1 Lesson 2
Exercise B

Interviewer: How is R&D activity measured and compared?

Expert: Well, there are various measures. Some analysts compare the budgets—both from government and from the private sector—that are available to R&D establishments.

Interviewer: So, the larger the budget, the higher the level of R&D activity.

Expert: Right. Others take into account the number of new patents that are filed and obtained by a company over a given time period. A third indicator that is sometimes used is the number and the frequency of publications—especially peer-reviewed publications—that are produced by a research organization.

Interviewer: What, in your opinion, is the best measure of R&D activity?

Expert: Well, to my mind, perhaps the best indicator is the percentage of revenues that a company spends on R&D each year. This is sometimes referred to as R&D intensity.

Interviewer: Why is this a good indicator of R&D activity?

Expert: Well, there are three reasons. Firstly this ratio—the percentage of revenue that is spent on R&D—is information that is regularly updated, secondly, this information is available to the public, and thirdly it reflects business risk.

Interviewer: Risk?

Expert: Yes. The extent to which a company is prepared to "gamble" on the future success of the products it is developing.

Unit 1, Lesson 2

CD
T-2

Exercise E

Interviewer: So how much do companies spend on R&D? That is, what sort of R&D intensity rates do we see, for example, in a typical U.S. manufacturing company?

Expert: Typical R&D expenditure might be around 3.5% of revenue—more or less.

Interviewer: As little as that?

Expert: Yes. High-tech companies, like computer manufacturers, for example, tend to spend more on R&D. Maybe around 7% of their revenue.

Interviewer: In which sectors do we find the bigger R&D spenders?

Expert: Well, these tend to be either high-tech companies or, especially, pharmaceutical companies. To give you an example, the American pharmaceutical giant Merck & Co. spends about 14% of revenue on R&D while the Swiss firm Novartis invests about 15% each year. Some telecommunications companies spend heavily on R&D. For example, the Swedish company Ericsson spends 25% of revenue on R&D.

Interviewer: And who is top of the list?

Expert: The biggest spender is the American pharmaceutical company Allergan. They spend an enormous amount on R&D—43% of revenue.

Unit 1, Lesson 3

CD
T-3

Exercise G

Manager: So, we need to choose someone to head up this new R&D project. It's a very important project and I want to make sure we choose the right person. Any ideas?

Assistant 1: Basically, we need someone who can coordinate the members of the team.

Assistant 2: Yes, but this person should also be someone who can motivate and lead people.

Manager: I agree. That's very important.

Assistant 1: Also, a good project leader must represent the group's interests in the larger organization. They should be a sort of champion for the project.

Assistant 2: Yes. Because it's the project leader who has to negotiate with management to obtain the resources that he or she needs to get the job done.

Assistant 1: We need a very responsible person because, in the end, it's the project leader who has to keep the project on schedule and within the budget.

Manager: You're right. That is also very important. So, who do you suggest?

Assistant 1: Well, I was thinking of . . . (fade)

Unit 1, Lesson 4

CD
T-4

Exercise B

Interviewer: How do you plan a research and development project?

R&D expert: We often use a system called the Critical Path Method or CPM.

Interviewer: How does that work?

R&D expert: Well, all projects are broken down into steps and sequences. Certain steps have to be completed before we can move on to the next one, while other steps can be done simultaneously. So we work out a logical sequence. Using the Critical Path Method, we can determine the minimum time we are going to need to complete the whole project.

Interviewer: So how does it work?

R&D expert: Well, we construct a diagram like this one here to show each step in the process and how long it will take to complete. For example, Step A will take two weeks, Step B one week, etc. Then we add up the total number of weeks of work to be completed. Once Step A is finished, work can start on Steps B, C, and D all at the same time, though, as you can see, Step C will take longer to finish. We can determine the earliest completion date for Project X by looking at all the possible paths through the diagram and finding the one that requires the most time. In this case, the longest path, that is, the "critical" path will take a total of ten weeks minimum from start to finish.

Interviewer: I see. So the Critical Path Method helps you to establish a timescale for a project.

R&D expert: That's right. But a CPM diagram like this also gives us other useful information. For example, in Project X, the earliest time we can begin Step H is eight weeks after the start, that is, once Steps A, C, and F have been finished. As we can see, Step B only needs one week and so it does not need to be started immediately in order to be finished on time. In other words, Step B has a couple of weeks of "slack time."

Interviewer: And how is this information useful?

R&D expert: It's useful because it allows us to allocate our resources more efficiently. We can keep the critical steps on schedule and, if necessary, postpone some of the slack steps without causing a delay to the whole project.

Interviewer: That way, the same people can work on different steps in the process.

R&D expert: Exactly, or the same equipment can be used for two different steps, for example. Of course, this diagram here is a very simple example just to give you an idea. In actual projects the relationships between the different parts are often very complex and a CPM diagram might cover a whole wall of my office!

Interviewer: But isn't it very time-consuming deciding on the sequence of the different tasks, estimating the time needed for each one, and drawing the diagrams?

R&D expert: Yes, it is time-consuming but we find that it is a great aid to planning and control. Of course, the job has been made a lot easier in recent years by special computer programs that can do critical path and slack time calculations for us.

Unit 1, Lesson 5
Exercise B
CD T-5

Lecturer: Okay, what is the essential role of an R&D

laboratory in industry? Well, basically it is to provide new products for manufacture and new or better processes for producing these products. Now, one very important issue for the people who plan these R&D projects is the relationship between development costs and projected sales.

In the early stages of a typical project, R&D expenditure is quite low. This gradually increases to a maximum point, holds steady at a sort of plateau, and then slowly declines, pretty much disappearing as early production problems are overcome and the product settles into its niche in the market. We can see this process here in Figure 1.

In a similar way, production and sales rise slowly at first, and then more rapidly, finally getting to a plateau. After a while, production starts to fall, with sales falling gradually as a product becomes obsolete. Alternatively, sales can sometimes decline quite abruptly if a product is replaced by a new one. This is illustrated here in Figure 2.

Ideally, of course, at any one time, a company will be handling a number of products—each one at a different stage in the cycle, some products in their initial stages of development, some that are just reaching their peak in terms of sales, and others that are now starting to decline. We can see this repeating cycle in Figure 3

Unit 1, Lesson 6
Exercise B
CD T-6

Interviewer: How do you develop a new product?

Expert: Well, first of all, of course, we need an idea.

Interviewer: Where do ideas come from?

Expert: Well, from many sources. Obviously, many ideas come from our own R&D department. But we also get ideas from other employees in the company, from our customers, from our competitors, from focus groups, from visiting trade shows… it varies. And we also use more formal idea-generating techniques, things like brainstorming, attribute listing, virtual prototyping, etc.

Interviewer: Okay, so you've got an idea. Now what?

Expert: Well, then we screen the ideas and get rid of any unsound concepts. We ask ourselves key questions about the ideas. We ask if the target market will benefit from a product, if it is technically feasible to manufacture it, and if it will be profitable. Sometimes, we test our ideas by asking a sample of prospective customers what they think of it.

Unit 1, Lesson 6
Exercise F
CD T-7

Interviewer: So, at this stage, you're still just discussing ideas, right?

Expert: Right. We call this whole "getting started" period the "fuzzy front end." It's usually not a very expensive part of the process but it can take up to 50% of total development time. This is where we decide on a clear sound concept and make serious commitments regarding time, money, and how the product will be.

Some people consider this phase as something that happens before development. But I prefer to think of it as an essential part of development and I include the time that we need for this as part of the total development cycle time.

Unit 2 Lesson 1
Exercise B

CD T-8
Narrator: Raymond Loewy was born in Paris, France in 1893. He obtained a degree in electrical engineering in 1918. One year later, he left France for the United States. He first worked as a fashion illustrator for Vogue magazine and also designed window displays for department stores in New York City.

In 1929, he received his first industrial design commission—to modernize the appearance of Gestetner's duplicating machine. Loewy's design was to remain unchanged for the next forty years. In the same year, Loewy started his own design firm.

In 1934, he designed the Coldspot refrigerator for Sears, Roebuck and Co. It was a great commercial success and it won first prize at the Paris International Exposition of 1937.

Starting in 1937, Loewy began working for the Pennsylvania Railroad, designing streamlined styling for their passenger trains. Over the following years, he designed various locomotives and passenger cars.

During the 1930s and 1940s, Loewy designed a wide range of household products with rounded corners and simplified lines such as the Frigidaire range of refrigerators and freezers. He made important contributions to the designs of electric shavers, toothbrushes, office machines, ballpoint pens, radios, bottles for soft drinks, packages, etc, etc.

In 1945, with five partners, he formed Raymond Loewy Associates, which was to become the largest industrial design firm in the world.

In 1954, he designed Greyhound's Scenicruiser bus.

In 1955, Loewy redesigned Coca-Cola's famous contour bottle adding the distinctive white lettering and in 1960 he designed Coca-Cola's first aluminum can.

In 1961, he designed the now classic Avanti sports car for Studebaker, for whom he had worked previously on other cars.

As a designer, Loewy's range was impressive. In 1964, he even designed a US postage stamp—the five-cent stamp featuring John F. Kennedy.

From 1967 to 1973, Loewy worked for NASA designing interiors for the Apollo and Skylab spacecraft.

In 1971, he designed the distinctive yellow and red Shell logo that is still used today.

Unit 2, Lesson 2
Exercise E

CD T-9
Speaker A: There is no single, unified style of industrial design but there are four trends that we can identify. One of these is a stress on impersonality in design—something that Peter Behrens was one of the first to establish. It is characterized by a certain neutrality of expression, whether a design comes from an individual or a group. In my opinion, this is just a natural part of mass production and marketing and it represents average taste.

Another trend we can see in industrial design is the way designers try to wrap or package products. Complex electronic or mechanical devices—perhaps designed by other engineers—have protective shells that keep them safe and clean and that also look neat and attractive.

There's also the continuing tendency to streamline designs. This design principle goes back to the 1930s with people like Raymond Loewy, who was a very influential industrial designer. Streamlined designs have contours designed to offer minimum resistance when moving through air or water. These designs are smooth and clean and extremely appealing to the eye.

The fourth trend I can identify is artificially accelerated obsolescence. This refers to the practice of changing a design intentionally to try to get people to replace the things they have with new ones. It's not just the design, of course. Advertising and changes in fashion play a large part as well. From an economic point of view, well, it's very effective.

Unit 2, Lesson 2
Exercise F

CD T-10
Speaker B: I agree with your list of the prevailing trends in industrial design. But, personally, I have doubts about a number of things. For example, this emphasis on impersonality. To me, it goes against individual expression—as if we all have to submit to "the machine."

As for the exterior packaging that covers up the engineering "insides" of a product, well, to me this is sort of superficial. I think some industrial designers spend too much time and money on this.

What you say about streamlining is true. People seem to like smooth, sleek lines. They suggest speed and movement. But, I think we've taken this trend to ridiculous extremes. I mean, why do we streamline things like toasters when they have nothing to do with movement or speed?

As for your last point, this is also true, regrettably. I can understand—and accept—the idea of artificially accelerated obsolescence in things that are just fashion items but I think it is unacceptable to try to persuade people to replace things like household appliances sooner than would usually be necessary as a result of normal wear and tear.

Unit 2, Lesson 4
CD T-11
Exercise B

Interviewer: What is value engineering?

Expert: It's a method by which a company tries to improve the value of its products.

Interviewer: How do you define "value"?

Expert: In business, value is the ratio of function to cost. Value can be increased either by improving function or by reducing cost. One of the basic principles in value engineering is that when trying to achieve better value, you do not make sacrifices in the quality of the product. Basically, what we as value engineers are trying to do is to optimize the balance of function and cost. We do this by looking for and identifying any expense that is unnecessary. This way, we improve the value of our products for us and for our customers.

Interviewer: Where did the concept of value engineering come from? Did someone invent it?

Expert: It sort of happened by accident. During the Second World War, General Electric suffered shortages of raw materials and parts for components. So they had to look for adequate substitutes. They found that in many cases, the use of substitute materials reduced production costs or improved a product or even produced both effects! So, what started as a necessity because of the war became part of company policy. Over time, this concept came to be known as value engineering.

Interviewer: So how do you apply value engineering to your products?

Expert: Basically, there are four main steps. First, we analyze the functions of a product and try to determine which functions are important. We ask questions like: What does this product have to do? What else could it do? What must this product not do?

Interviewer: Okay, then what?

Expert: Well, then we think of alternatives. We ask ourselves: What other ways could we achieve the same result? What else will give us the function we want? Then, thirdly, we evaluate all the alternatives and compare them with the product as it actually is and we work out how much we would save if we did

things a different way. Then, lastly, we chose the best option and present our findings and recommendations to the production department.

Unit 2, Lesson 5
CD T-12
Exercise B

Interviewer: Your company designs and produces computer games. How do you test your products before putting them out in the market?

Expert: It's simple. We conduct playtests. This means, basically, that one of our software designers—or someone else—tests a new game for bugs and improvements. Playtests are very common now for all sorts of games—an established part of the quality control process.

Interviewer: So how do you organize a playtest?

Expert: Well, there are three basic types of playtest that we can do. There's "open," "closed," or "beta."

Interviewer: And what are the differences between the three types?

Expert: Well, an open playtest, as the name suggests, is pretty much open to anyone who wishes to join. Some people use this term for when a company recruits testers from outside. A closed playtest, on the other hand, is an internal testing process that is not available to the public at all.

Interviewer: And "beta" tests?

Expert: Well, beta testing usually takes place in the final stages just before we go to market with a new product. Beta testing is usually semi-open and we do it with a limited form of the game just to pick up any last-minute problems.

Unit 2, Lesson 5
CD T-13
Exercise H

Narrator: Companies have discovered that "eating their own dog food" offers four primary benefits: Firstly, product developers are familiar with using the products that they develop.

Secondly, other company employees acquire firsthand knowledge of and experience with the company's own products.

Thirdly, product users can see that the company has confidence in its own products.

Lastly, technically knowledgeable employees, working in perhaps a very wide range of business situations, are able to discover and report any bugs in a product before it is released to the general public.

Unit 2, Lesson 6
CD T-14
Exercise B

Interviewer: First of all, could you clarify the difference between safety testing and performance testing?

Expert: Well, unlike safety testing, which is usually mandatory, independent performance testing is a voluntary process. It is dictated just by the goals and objectives of the company.

Interviewer: I see. So, if it's voluntary, why would a company choose to performance test its products?

Expert: There are many reasons. One simple benefit is that it enables a company to verify its own internal test data. But there are a number of other very sound business reasons. In fact, in addition to safety testing, independent performance testing offers one of the best ways to gain a demonstrable competitive edge over the competition

Interviewer: How?

Expert: Well, by doing performance testing, a company can measure how well its products compare with those of its competitors so that it can design them to be more competitive.

Interviewer: I see.

Expert: Another benefit is that after conducting performance testing, a company can make impressive marketing claims such as "the longest lasting . . ." or "the world's quietest . . ." or "the most economical in its class," etc.

Interviewer: Claims which can have great impact on customers.

Expert: Exactly. Validated performance tests also help a company to secure valuable approval and endorsements from trade associations in their industry.

Interviewer: Which are also worth having.

Expert: And if a company has conducted independent performance tests, it can show to retailers that its products are the best in their class.

🔘 Unit 3 Lesson 1
CD T-15 Exercise C

Narrator: Industrial engineers manage the layout and the design of industrial and manufacturing facilities. They try to achieve the most advantageous and efficient deployment of the site and the machinery. They schedule and direct the placement and the flow of raw materials, components, and machine parts. They organize personnel and equipment and try to optimize the use of human resources. They supervise the running of the plant and ensure that the whole operation runs safely.

🔘 Unit 3, Lesson 1
CD T-16 Exercise E

Narrator: Industrial engineers have to have expert knowledge in a wide variety of different fields. The areas of expertise that are particularly relevant are:

facility layout and design, machinery and equipment, materials and components, production planning and methods, logistics and operations research, statistics, ergonomics which are interactions between human beings and machines, human resources, safety procedures, management, and cost issues.

🔘 Unit 3, Lesson 2
CD T-17 Exercise B

Speaker 1: This company makes household goods. Currently, I'm working on a motor for a new washing machine.

Speaker 2: At the moment, I'm working on a system that will help companies handle and switch telephone calls more quickly.

Speaker 3: The company I work for specializes in products that are ergonomically designed. I supervise the manufacture of keyboards that reduce the risk of strain and injury to users.

Speaker 4: I work in R&D. I'm looking at ways to make generators and turbines that are more efficient and easy to maintain.

🔘 Unit 3, Lesson 2
CD T-18 Exercise D

Speaker 5: I work for a company that produces radar and navigation systems for ships. We do a lot of work for the Navy.

Speaker 6: This company makes components for the automobile industry. Right now, I am working on a device that monitors engine functions.

Speaker 7: I design monitors. I am creating a new, cheaper flat-screen monitor.

Speaker 8: I work for an electric utility company. I operate the transmission devices at the power station.

🔘 Unit 3, Lesson 3
CD T-19 Exercise D

Interviewer: What is your job?

Claudia: I'm a computer systems software engineer.

Interviewer: And what do you do exactly?

Claudia: I coordinate the construction and maintenance of a company's computer systems.

Interviewer: Do you work here at SysTech or outside?

Claudia: A bit of both. I'm here some of the time but I also spend a lot of time on site configuring and installing computer systems at a company.

Interviewer: What sort of things do you do for a company?

Claudia: Well, companies have various needs. They have to organize things like ordering, inventory, billing, payroll, etc. I help companies to coordinate their computer systems in these departments.

Interviewer: Do you actually write software programs?

Claudia: No, not really. As a software engineer, I need to have good programming skills, but I'm more concerned with developing algorithms and analyzing and solving programming problems than with actually writing code programs.

Interviewer: What else do you do?

Claudia: I also help companies to set up their intranet systems and, in general, I make suggestions about the technical direction of a company and I help them to plan for future growth.

Unit 3, Lesson 4
CD T-20 **Exercise C**

Engineer: With all unit processes, you have to have good knowledge of chemical reactions and you need to know the basic laws concerning the conservation of matter and the conservation of energy as well as principles of chemical equilibrium.

The chemical engineer has to select and specify the chemical processes and the most appropriate equipment that will best meet the particular requirements of production.

What was a challenge for me at first was moving from the laboratory to large-scale industrial production. It's totally different.

Chemical engineers must organize all the unit processes in their correct sequence.

And, of course, they must take into account the economic cost of the whole process.

Unit 3, Lesson 4
CD T-21 **Exercise E**

Engineer: Because continuous or assembly-line operations are more efficient and economical than batch processes and lend themselves to automatic control, chemical engineers were among the first to incorporate automatic controls into their designs.

Unit 3, Lesson 6
CD T-22 **Exercise A**

Interviewer: Different fields of engineering often overlap. Which engineering disciplines are more closely related to mechanical engineering?

Engineer 1: There are a number of fields, including electrical engineering, civil engineering, industrial engineering, systems engineering, aerospace engineering, and nuclear engineering.

Interviewer: How would you define mechanical engineering? That is, what is the nature of the work?

Engineer 2: As mechanical engineers, we research, develop, design, manufacture, and test all sorts of tools, machines, engines, and other mechanical devices. I should mention that mechanical engineers also design tools that other engineers need for their work.

Interviewer: What are the basic theoretical subjects that a mechanical engineer has to be conversant with?

Engineer 3: There are many things . . . I would say that the basic areas of knowledge are dynamics, statics, solid mechanics, strength of materials, fluid dynamics, thermodynamics, heat transfer, kinematics, mechatronics . . .

Interviewer: What sorts of things do mechanical engineers actually make?

Engineer 4: Well, the list is almost endless. Mechanical engineers make machines for producing power—things like electric generators, steam or gas turbines—and different types of internal combustion engines. They also make machines that use power—things like air-conditioning and refrigeration equipment, machine tools, elevators and escalators, even robots . . .

Unit 4 Lesson 1
CD T-23 **Exercise H**

Interviewer: What happened in the immediate aftermath of the *Challenger* accident?

Spokesperson: In early February 1986, President Ronald Reagan announced the creation of a Presidential Commission on the Space Shuttle *Challenger* Accident.

Interviewer: Known to most people as the Rogers Commission, right?

Spokesperson: That's right. The chairman of the commission was William P. Rogers. At the same time, NASA established the *Challenger* Data and Design Analysis Task Force to support the work of the Commission.

Interviewer: How long did the investigation take?

Spokesperson: It took four months to complete and required the involvement of more than 6,000 people. The report was published and delivered to the president early June 1986.

Unit 4, Lesson 1
CD T-24 **Exercise I**

Interviewer: So what changes were made as a result of the commission's report?

Spokesman: Well, modifications were made both to shuttle hardware and to NASA's safety and quality assurance procedures. While the space shuttle fleet was grounded, hundreds of modifications were incorporated into the shuttle system. The SRBs were completely redesigned and a new joint design was subjected to stringent examination and review. NASA put the main space shuttle engines through the most thorough ground-testing program in their history. This was the equivalent in operational time to more than 36 real missions. All engine improvements were certified to demonstrate improved reliability and operating safety margins.

Interviewer: I see.

Spokesman: And, as I mentioned, apart from making changes to hardware, NASA completely reorganized its safety programs. The Office of Safety, Reliability, Maintainability, and Quality Assurance was established in 1986. This has direct authority for safety and quality control for all NASA operations.

Unit 4, Lesson 2
CD T-25
Exercise B

Engineer #1: I work as a maintenance engineer. I am responsible for the continued safe and dependable operation of the equipment in the plant where I work and for carrying out timely and efficient repairs.

Engineer #2: I work in the field of safety engineering. Basically, our main objective is the prevention of accidents. We develop methods and procedures to safeguard workers, especially those who work in hazardous occupations.

Engineer #3: As an operating engineer, I oversee and control a number of different areas at this factory: machinery, power, transportation, communications. I have to set up procedures and supervise personnel to ensure that the operation runs in a reliable and economic way.

Engineer #4: I'm a quality control engineer. It is my job to carry out on-site inspections to check that all parts and systems meet various technical and other requirements. Of course, these may also cover safety issues.

Unit 4, Lesson 3
CD T-26
Exercise B

Stephanie: Hi. I'm Stephanie. I'm a civil engineer. I'm currently working on a large tunnel project in the north of the country. We don't have to wear any special clothes but strong boots are recommended. I'm often working close to cranes and other big machines so I have to wear a hard hat at all times. When we work at night, I have to wear a special vest with reflective material so that people can see me.

Greg: My name is Greg. I'm a radiologist. At the moment I am doing some research into the use of X-rays and gamma rays in the diagnosis and treatment of disease. In my work I handle radioactive material. To avoid exposure to harmful radiation, we have to wear

protective clothing and, sometimes we work behind a protective screen. We must not be exposed to radiation for long periods and so there are strict time controls.

Carol: My name is Carol. I'm an electronic engineer. In my present job, I manufacture LEDs. The components are very small and delicate. They can be damaged by just one speck of dust. Everything in my workplace must be extremely clean. So I have to work in a clean room, which is a space where the particles in the air and the humidity are strictly controlled. We mustn't let any dust or moisture come into contact with the components. So I have to wear a special suit with a mask over my mouth and vinyl gloves. When we're not in the clean room, we can wear our normal clothes.

Tom: My name's Tom. I'm a production engineer. At the moment I'm coordinating the installation of heavy machinery at a new car manufacturing plant. Factories are very noisy places so one thing that is essential in this place is earplugs, which you must use to prevent serious damage to your hearing. Oh, and your hard hat. You have to wear a hard hat at all times. There is no real dress code where I work. I mean, you don't have to wear a tie. Of course, you can if you want to but I normally don't bother.

Unit 4, Lesson 4
CD T-27
Exercise B

Narrator: The Tacoma Narrows Bridge was built in July 1940 across the Narrows of Puget Sound in the state of Washington. Its 2,800-foot span made it the world's third longest bridge at that time. But the bridge would only be in operation for four months. Soon after its opening, it was discovered that the bridge swayed and buckled dangerously in windy conditions. The bridge buckled along its length, i.e., one half of the central span would rise as the other half went down.

Then engineers noticed a different type of twisting that they had never seen before. The left side of the bridge would go down as the right side would lift up, while the centerline of the road would remain motionless.

What actually brought the bridge crashing down was another type of twisting in which the midpoint of the bridge stayed still while the two halves of the bridge twisted in opposite directions.

The collapse of the bridge was not due to just resonance problems or just aerodynamic problems but, rather, a combination of the two effects. Torsional disturbance caused the effects of the wind to increase, which, in turn, caused more twisting and so on. The amplitude of the motion gradually increased until it was too strong for the supporting cables and they snapped. The failure of the Tacoma Narrows Bridge acted as a spur to research in aerodynamic design and since that time, all new bridges have been modeled in wind tunnels prior to construction.

Unit 4, Lesson 5

CD T-28 **Exercise E**

Interviewer: Could you explain the PDCA cycle for us?

Expert: Sure. It's really quite simple. The cycle begins with the letter *P*. *P* is for Plan. In this stage, you establish your objectives and the processes that are necessary to produce the results you're looking for, according to your specifications.

Interviewer: Okay. *P* is for Plan. What next?

Expert: What next? *D* for Do! This is when you implement the process, set it into motion.

Interviewer: Next is *C*. I imagine that this stands for Check, am I right?

Expert: Exactly. This is the time for monitoring and evaluating your results against your initial objectives and specifications and also the time to report these results.

Interviewer: Okay. Got it. Finally, I guess *A* is for Act, right?

Expert: That's right. Now you act upon your results. This involves reviewing all of the four steps and making any necessary modifications and improvements to the process before its next implementation which, ideally, should take place as soon as possible.

Unit 4, Lesson 6

CD T-29 **Exercise C**

Narrator: Statistical quality control techniques usually produce positive results that are shown in increased sales and profits. However, sometimes, despite the implementation of a quality control program, sales keep on falling. The most common reason for this is that the original product specifications do not sufficiently take into account the most important factor, which is what the customer requires. Remember, if the original specifications do not reflect the correct quality requirements, it's no good trying to inspect or manufacture quality into a finished product. The three most common characteristics that tend to be neglected are reliability, maintainability, and safety.

Unit 5 Lesson 1

CD T-30 **Exercise B**

Interviewer: You've worked as an engineer and have written about engineering for many years. What trends do you see in engineering today and for the future?

Expert: Well, one area that has grown in importance in recent years is time-study engineering. More and more, people have come to realize that engineers need to work not just with machines but also with people.

Interviewer: How do you mean?

Expert: Well, for example, to find out how machines can be operated most efficiently by operators. You see, a small change in the position of the controls on a machine or even in the way the operator makes certain muscle movements can have a big effect on speed, efficiency, and production.

Interviewer: I see.

Expert: Another related field that has developed over the last twenty years or so is human-factors engineering, which some people also call ergonomics.

Interviewer: And what do human-factors engineers do exactly?

Expert: They work to establish criteria for the efficient, safe, human-centered design of things like the large, complex control panels that direct and monitor operations in, for example, a nuclear reactor.

Interviewer: What other changes have you seen in your profession over recent years?

Expert: One interesting trend is the development of an interdisciplinary approach

Interviewer: What do you mean by "interdisciplinary"? The idea of specialists from various engineering disciplines working together?

Expert: Yes, but an interdisciplinary approach can also include experts from legal, social, behavioral, and environmental fields as well. I think we'll see this trend continue and grow in the future.

Interviewer: What trends have you seen regarding the engineering profession itself?

Expert: Well, one of the most important recent trends in the engineering profession is licensure. Today, many engineers are licensed by the state, just as doctors and lawyers are. The construction of public and commercial structures needs approval by a professionally licensed engineer, especially in cases where public and worker safety is a consideration.

Unit 5, Lesson 2

CD T-31 **Exercise C**

Narrator: If you ask a hundred people in the street to say what image the word "scientist" evokes in their minds, what do they describe? A person in a white coat and wearing thick eyeglasses working with beakers and test tubes full of bubbling liquids in some university laboratory. A stereotype, of course. For one thing, scientists do not just work in academia. Many are found in private industry or working for government agencies.

Most scientists in the private sector are involved with applied research and development. Of course, private-sector scientists and scientists employed at universities both deal with the same concepts. But if you are working in the private sector, you are coping with more stringent timeframes and you are more attuned to the bottom line—money. If you are an engineer, you are probably working closer to an actual production line, using resources to make products within a budget and a timetable.

If you are a physicist, you could be hired by a biotechnology firm or you could find yourself working for a semiconductor manufacturer. If you are a chemist, you might find yourself working for a pharmaceutical company, a paint manufacturer, or a food-processing company. If your field is biology, you could work in the biomedical field researching and developing new drugs, vaccines, and treatments.

If you have completed a degree in science or engineering, you have proved that you can think analytically and that you are comfortable with math. If you have gotten this far, you have mastered a host of scientific theories and terminology that are incomprehensible to most laypeople. But if you want to do well in today's world, learn how to work in a team and how to communicate effectively, especially with people from other fields or with laypeople. If you are looking for a bigger budget for your research project, make sure you have the communication skills necessary to argue your case with the people who hold the purse strings.

Unit 5, Lesson 3
CD T-32 **Exercise C**

Narrator: While women represent half of the population of the United States, they make up only 10% of the country's physicists, just 9% of its engineers, and only 20% of its engineering students. Engineering is still a male-dominated profession, although women's participation in the engineering workforce has increased dramatically over the last 25 years. Some engineering disciplines have a higher percentage of women professionals than others. For example, 14% of chemical engineers, 11% of industrial engineers, 9% of civil engineers, and 7% of electrical engineers are women.

Unit 5, Lesson 3
CD T-33 **Exercise G**

Interviewer: So you think we should be encouraging more girls and young women to become engineers. Why?

Engineer: Well, I believe that a more diverse engineering community offers benefits for society in general.

Interviewer: What do you mean by that?

Engineer: What I mean is that women can bring different

perspectives to problem-solving and offer different approaches to teamwork. This can enable project teams to generate more creative solutions and to address society's needs better.

Interviewer: I see.

Engineer: And there are also benefits from a business point of view.

Interviewer: For example?

Engineer: Well, it makes good business sense for companies to engage women in research, design, and development. Think about it—women represent at least 50% of the population and they are a major consumer group. If companies can attract women engineers, then they can gain a better understanding of their customers' needs, they can improve the design of their products, and they can compete more effectively in the marketplace.

Unit 5, Lesson 5
CD T-34 **Exercise G**

Narrator: Median annual earnings of aerospace engineers in 2002 were $72,750. The middle 50 percent earned between $59,520 and $88,310. The lowest 10 percent earned less than $49,640, and the highest 10 percent earned more than $105,060.

According to a 2003 salary survey by the National Association of Colleges and Employers, bachelor's degree candidates in aerospace engineering received starting salary offers averaging $48,028 a year, master's degree candidates were offered $61,162, and Ph.D. candidates were offered $68,406.

Unit 5, Lesson 6
CD T-35 **Exercise D**

Engineer: As for the career outlook for engineering over the next ten years or so, well, I don't claim to have all the answers but I expect to see an increase in opportunities but this will be slower than in other occupations Why? Because many engineers tend to work in slow-growing manufacturing industries and this can hold down their employment growth. However, overall job opportunities in engineering should be quite good because graduate numbers appear to be in balance with the number of jobs that will be available.

Companies are aware of competitive pressures and advancing technology and they know that they need to improve and update product designs and optimize their manufacturing processes. New computer and communications systems have improved the design process and promise to continue doing so. Some people insist that computer technologies threaten to limit employment opportunities. Personally, I refuse to accept this point of view.